"The health advantages of a plant-strong diet are compelling and well proven. But preparing yummy meals that are wholesome can be time consuming. That's where this book comes in. Slow cookers can be huge labor and time savers, if you know how to use them. This is the book that will show you how."

—John Robbins, author of *The Food Revolution*, *The New Good Life*, *Diet for a New America*, and other bestsellers

THE VEGAN SLOW COOKER

Simply Set It and Go with 150 Recipes for Intensely Flavorful, Fuss-Free Fare Everyone (Vegan or Not!) Will Devour

KATHY HESTER

FAIR WINDS
PRESS
BEVERLY, MASSACHUSETTS

© 2011 Fair Winds Press
Text © 2011 Kathy Hester
Photography © 2011 Fair Winds Press

First published in the USA in 2011 by
Fair Winds Press, a member of
Quayside Publishing Group
100 Cummings Center
Suite 406-L
Beverly, MA 01915-6101
www.fairwindspress.com

17 16 15 14 13   11 12 13 14

ISBN-13: 978-1-59233-464-3
ISBN-10: 1-59233-464-4

Digital edition published in 2011
eISBN-13: 978-1-61058-155-4

Library of Congress Cataloging-in-Publication Data available

Book design by bradhamdesign.com
Book layout by meganjonesdesign.com
Photography by Bill Bettencourt

Printed and bound in China

To all my friends who taught me
that anything you put your mind to
is possible with a little love and support.

And to my companion animals,
past and present, who showed me
how to wholeheartedly throw myself
into any endeavor that's worth doing.

CONTENTS

INTRODUCTION
SLOW COOKER LOVE

I inherited my first slow cooker from my mother. When I was a very poor grad student, it became the center of my kitchen. I could eat for half the price by cooking everything from scratch. Plus, it cooked while I was in class. I managed to stay within my food budget and feed all my friends most nights, too.

A versatile appliance, the slow cooker goes way beyond preconceived limitations. It can even stand in for a rice cooker or an oven in a pinch. It's a great way to extend your kitchen during the holidays, and it can double as a buffet server, too.

Because I work all day, it allows me to either come home to a ready-to-eat meal or prepare one as soon as I get home. I like to make some of the 2-hour dishes after work, then go for a walk or do a few chores around the house while it's cooking. The best part is that neither way requires me to be in the kitchen the whole cooking time.

In the winter I cook breakfast in it, and I usually come home to a hearty stew. But people often forget that it puts off very little heat and is a perfect addition to your kitchen in the summer as well. Impress your friends with focaccia or pizza from the slow cooker and a simple salad on a summer's evening.

Another unexpected place to use your slow cooker is camping. It's not so good for backpackers, but it's perfect for car or RV camping. You can even buy slow cookers that run on 12 volts and cook right in your car! I love coming back from a hike or swim to a big pot of jambalaya to eat by the fire.

The slow cooker is a perfect tool for a vegan kitchen. Instead of buying cans of beans, you can cook yours without all the salt while you're at work or asleep. Soups and stews really meld well together after cooking all day, and you can even make pasta and rice dishes in it. You may just find yourself as enamored with your slow cooker as I am with mine. But try not to accumulate as many slow cookers as I have. People will start to talk!

CHAPTER 1

SLOW COOKER BASICS

There are a few misconceptions about the slow cooker, one being that it's just to cook meat. Nothing could be further from the truth!

A slow cooker is the perfect tool in a vegan arsenal. I wouldn't be able to eat as many home-made meals without it. It's great for making soups and stews in the winter. But it also has its place in a summer kitchen. Most of us still eat hot foods in the summertime, and a slow cooker is a great way to keep your house from heating up. You can even make a pizza in it!

If you work a day job, imagine dinner waiting when you walk in the door. It's the same case if you are a stay-at-home parent or a college student. The slow cooker buys time to focus on other things in our lives and still have a nice, nutritious meal.

A little over half the recipes in this book cook from 6 to 8 hours. Many others are 2 to 4 hours. The shorter cooking time is perfect for when you want to come home, start dinner, and do some chores, go to the gym, or relax for a while before you eat.

SLOW COOKER BASICS

People think that with a slow cooker you just throw in a few things and magically you get a tasty meal. While it really is simple to cook in one, you still need to get a few basic safety concepts under your belt.

STAY AT HOME THE FIRST TIME YOU USE YOUR SLOW COOKER

As you would with any appliance that heats up, you need to check and make sure the slow cooker is functioning properly before using it without being in the house. This will also let you know whether it runs on the hotter side, so you can adjust recipes with no mishaps.

FILL YOUR SLOW COOKER TO THE MANUFACTURER'S RECOMMENDED AMOUNT

Your slow cooker should be half to three-fourths full to cook at its proper temperature. This can vary from model to model as well as make to make. Be sure to check your user guide to see what's recommended for your model. You may find that foods such as stews and casseroles burn if this rule is not followed, because the food will cook much hotter than it should. This is one of the main complaints about newer slow cookers. If you have a 6- to 7-quart (5.7 to 6.6 L) slow cooker, you can double many of the recipes to fill your slow cooker up enough.

Note: We will use this to our advantage in some of the baking recipes, by not filling the slow cooker up to the recommended fill line.

USE COMMON SENSE

Always make sure the area around the sides of the slow cooker is clear. I leave my slow cooker on while I'm away at work at least three to five times a week. It's made to leave on while you are away from the house. But the outside parts do get hot, so you do not want it near anything that could melt or overheat. If you have young children, make sure the slow cooker is where little toddler hands can't grab the hot parts or pull on the cord.

CHECK THE SETTINGS ON YOUR SLOW COOKER

Almost all slow cookers have a low and high setting, and many have a warming setting as well. Some of the fancier slow cookers have programmable settings. You can't program when the slow cooker starts, but you can program how long it will cook at your chosen setting (low or high). After the allotted time, the slow cooker will switch to warm to keep your food ready to eat once you get home.

One thing to be aware of is an auto setting that is found on some slow cookers. From one of my amazing recipe testers, I found out that, at least in Canada, there is an auto temperature instead of low on some slow cookers. This is not the timing mechanism that controls switching the setting to warm after the programmed time. It is actually on the dial in place of the low. This auto setting cooks the first 2 hours on high and them automatically switches the cooker to low. You need to treat this like a very hot slow cooker and reduce total times and add extra liquid in most dishes. The 2 hours on high are like 4 on low.

KNOW YOUR SLOW COOKER

Older slow cookers cook at lower temperatures than newer models do. With all the food safety concerns of the past few years, slow cooker manufacturers have raised the temperature at which their appliances cook. The new low is almost as hot as the old high! If your slow cooker runs on the hotter side, you will have more evaporation and will need to add extra liquid to make up for this.

If you have an older model that cooks at a lower temperature, you may need less liquid and/or longer cooking times. Newer models may need extra liquid and tend to cook quicker than the older ones do.

Once you cook a few dishes, you'll have a good idea what temperature your slow cooker cooks at. Until then, use caution and add more liquid rather than less. You can always cook something longer, but if it burns it's not always as easy to fix it.

SLOW COOKER Q & A

I have ten slow cookers and I'm not afraid to use them. Experimenting with them has given me a depth of knowledge that can help you on your own slow cooker journey. Here are a few of the questions I get asked the most. You might find a few tips that will make it easier and tastier to cook in your slow cooker.

Q: HOW CAN I TELL WHETHER MY SLOW COOKER RUNS HOTTER?

A: If you find that gravies or sauces don't thicken as instructed, you probably have an older one. If you can see that your soup is almost at a boil on high, then you have a slow cooker that runs hot. There is no good or bad here; you just need to learn how to adjust cooking times and liquid amounts so all your dishes turn out perfect.

Q: WHAT'S THE DIFFERENCE BETWEEN A SLOW COOKER AND A CROCK-POT?

A: They are two words for exactly the same thing. Crock-Pot is a brand name that's become interchangeable with the item name, just like tissues have come to be known as Kleenex. With that said, there are many differences among brands, types, and years of manufacture of slow cookers.

Q: WHAT SIZE SLOW COOKER SHOULD I USE?

A: It really depends on how many people you cook for, and how much leftovers you like to have. Most of the recipes in this book work great in a 4-quart (3.8 L) slow cooker, unless another size is clearly noted, and tend to serve four to six. You can easily double, or even triple, most of the recipes in this book to fit properly in a larger slow cooker.

Q: WHAT'S THE BEST SLOW COOKER FOR ME?

A: There is no right answer to this one. It depends on your family size, and how simple or complex you like your gadgets to be. An inexpensive 4-quart (3.8 L) with manual controls will work just as well as a more expensive model with a programmable timer. A 4-quart (3.8 L) size can work for two people with leftovers or make a single meal for a family of four or five. A 6- or 7-quart (5.7 or 6.6 L) will feed eight to twelve people, depending on the dish.

If you have unpredictable work times it might be worth the extra money to get a pro-grammable one. It doesn't let you put off cooking until a certain time, but it does switch to warm after the time in the allotted time has elapsed. This can save your dinner if you come home a few hours later than planned.

I recommend that everyone pick up a small 1½- to 2-quart (1.4 to 1.9 L) slow cooker for breakfast and party dips. They are very inexpensive, and I promise you'll use it more than you think. I have two that I use weekly. You can also buy a 3-in-1 slow cooker that has three crocks: 2-quart (1.9 L), 4-quart (3.8 L), and 6-quart (5.7 L). It's great if you don't have a lot of storage room because they nest inside each other.

Q: WHY PRECOOK ONIONS, GARLIC, ETC.? CAN I SKIP THAT STEP?

A: You can skip the step, but the dish will not be as flavorful. Do I ever skip it? Heck, yeah! If I'm in a hurry and it's the difference between eating a home-cooked meal or grabbing takeout on the way home, I throw everything in together.

I've set up most recipes so that you can do most of the prep the night before, including softening onions and other veggies. Getting most of the prep done the night before really makes cooking in the morning much easier.

Q: DO I NEED TO DO ANYTHING DIFFERENT TO SEASON FOOD IN THE SLOW COOKER?

A: Because there is a long cooking time, you should always taste the dish before you serve it. Reseason, if needed. You'll find that you will do this especially with stews and soups. Really, if you get in the habit of doing this you'll find out it helps make any cooking method taste better.

Add or readjust fresh herbs right before serving. For example, if you are using fresh ginger in a dish and cook it all day, you may need to add a little more ginger about 30 minutes before serving.

INGREDIENT SUBSTITUTIONS

I'm notorious for using what I have on hand in place of what's called for in a recipe, and I don't expect you to be any different.

CANNED VS. HOMEMADE

I've listed measurements for canned beans and homemade wherever possible (see recipe on page 17). Beans are super easy to make in the slow cooker. You can make them with no added salt, and you can make sure they are organic.

If you're trying to avoid BPA in cans, make the recipe to freeze your own diced tomatoes (see recipe on page 25) to use in place of canned. This also works for canned pumpkin and butternut squash. Just use 1½ cups (368 g) precooked puréed pumpkin (see recipe on page 34) or squash instead.

MAIN INGREDIENT SUBSTITUTIONS

If a recipe calls for tofu and you're trying to avoid soy, try using homemade or store-bought seitan instead. Going gluten-free? Then add beans or tofu in place of seitan. Almost every recipe can work well with a switch like this. Even the Tempeh Braised with Figs and Port Wine (page 123) could work great with white beans in place of the tempeh.

SMOKY FLAVORS

Can't find liquid smoke where you live? It's showing up more in stores outside of the South, but if it hasn't hit your area yet, add some smoked paprika, smoked salt, or chipotle chile powder. You'll need to start on the light side, and then add more to your taste. After all, you don't want to make your food too hot or salty. You can order liquid smoke from stores on the Internet. It's actually an inexpensive item. It's vegan and has no added chemicals!

HERBS

I'm in love with cutting celery and lovage. They are great to use in place of celery, and don't take up as much room in the fridge. In pots they stay fairly small, but planted in the garden they can grow much larger.

Dried and fresh herbs can always be switched out. Just use 1 tablespoon fresh for each teaspoon dried, or vice versa.

SPICES

A few of the dishes call for some spices that might not already be in your cupboard. To try new spices I recommend that you go to a store that sells bulk spices. You can get as little or as much as you want and they are much cheaper than at the supermarket. It's great for your budget.

BOUILLON VS. BROTH

I almost always use bouillon in recipes instead of broth. It takes less space to store and can add a quick flavor boost to stir-fries, loaves, and other dishes when broth would make them too soupy. If you prefer to use broth, just leave out the bouillon and use broth instead of the liquids called for in that recipe.

GLUTEN-FREE SUBSTITUTIONS

In most of the recipes you can use gluten-free baking mix. You can also use oat flour in place of oat bran if you can't find a gluten-free version in your area. Bob's Red Mill (www.bobsredmill.com) is a great resource for gluten-free products and even has nutritional yeast that is gluten-free.

STEEL-CUT OATS VS. ROLLED OATS

Everyone has his or her favorite, but the slow cooker does better with steel-cut oats. It's the longer cooking time that makes them work well.

If you don't like steel-cut oats, try using polenta, grits, or plain brown rice in the breakfast recipes. It's a great change of pace, and you may find yourself a new favorite.

SWEETENERS

Personally, I use tons of different sweeteners. I find that each one lends its unique properties to different kinds of dishes. Agave nectar and maple syrup are pretty interchangeable and you won't need to make many adjustments to the recipe. If you swap agave nectar for brown sugar, you will need to use less liquid in the recipe to make up for that.

If you are using a sweetener that is not called for, check the consistency of the batter or mixture and adjust accordingly. More liquid or more flour may be needed.

NONDAIRY CREAMER AND MILK

When I call for nondairy creamer, I am not suggesting that you go get one of those artificial coffee whiteners. I'm talking about a soy or coconut creamer that you'll find in the refrigerated section of the supermarket with soy, rice, and coconut milk.

You can always use your standby nondairy milk in place of creamer. It just won't be quite as rich. Most of the recipes in this book have been tested with soy, rice, almond, or coconut milk (the So Delicious brand in the carton—not the canned kind). You should be able to use hemp or oat milk as well.

CHAPTER 2

STAPLES YOU'LL WANT TO KNOW: MAKE YOUR OWN BOUILLON, SEITAN, SAUCES, AND MORE

This chapter is by far my favorite part of the book, because it contains many of the recipes that keep my food budget under control. It allows me to avoid the BPA in canned foods, as well as the ever-rising high prices on vegan staples such as bouillon, sausage, and seitan. These are recipes that you'll find yourself using time and time again.

Make an effort to plan one day a week (or month) to stock your freezer with beans, seitan, and bouillon. That way, you'll always have some on hand, and you'll avoid those extra trips to the grocery. You'll save money, too. For example, one 15-ounce (420 g) can of beans costs three to six times as much as a single 1-pound (455 g) bag of beans. Cooking the 1 pound (454 g) of beans yields the amount of cooked beans you'd get in three or four cans! One 22-ounce (615 g) bag of wheat gluten flour costs about the same as four frozen chicken-style seitan patties. That one bag of flour will make dozens. That's worth part of a quiet Sunday afternoon to me. Happy cooking!

1. Dry Beans from Scratch
2. Perfectly Easy Everyday Brown Rice
3. Chickeny Bouillon
4. Beefy Bouillon
5. Chick'n Seitan
6. Beefy Seitan
7. Apple Sage Sausage
8. Tea-Scented Tofu
9. Preserve-the-Harvest Diced Tomatoes
10. Beyond-Easy Baked Potatoes
11. All-Occasion Roasted Garlic
12. Citrus Rum BBQ Sauce
13. Balsamic Onion Marmalade
14. Homemade Smoky Ketchup
15. Fall Harvest Fruit Butter
16. Perfect Pumpkin Purée
17. Brandied Cranberry Sauce

DRY BEANS FROM SCRATCH

▶ SOY-FREE ▶ GLUTEN-FREE

If you're picky about what goes into your food, making beans from scratch is perfect for you. You can control how much salt, if any, goes into them. Even better, dry beans cost three to six times less than canned, so you're saving money, too! Use any kind of bean other than lentils or split peas; they cook much quicker, so you will cook them in a dish, not in advance.

INGREDIENTS:

1 pound (454 g) dried beans

A WORTHY NOTE

- Cook extra beans and freeze in bags to use later. I freeze mine in 1½-cup (340 g) portions so that it's easy to switch out a bag for a can of beans.

- Though all dry beans may look alike, beans that have been on the shelf (or in your pantry) a long time can take up to twice as long to cook completely. However, there is nothing wrong with eating them once they're cooked.

- Split peas and lentils cook much faster than larger beans such as pinto, black, and white. They are often cooked in a recipe dry, while the larger beans are cooked before they are added to other recipes.

- You can cook any beans in the slow cooker, but be aware that kidney beans can have a toxin called *phytohaemagglutinin* and need to be brought up to a boiling temperature to destroy the toxin. So boil them for 10 minutes before cooking in the slow cooker. This step is not necessary for other types of beans.

DIRECTIONS:

Rinse the beans, and make sure there are no little rocks that might have been missed. Place in the slow cooker and add water to come about 3 inches (7.5 cm) above the beans Cook on low overnight, or for 6 to 8 hours.

After you cook the beans once in your slow cooker, you'll be able to determine whether you need to use less water (about 2 inches [5 cm], instead of 3 inches [7.5 cm]). It will vary depending on how hot your slow cooker runs. Use a slotted spoon to remove the beans if there is extra water.

YIELD: 4½ to 5 cups (788 to 875 g)
TOTAL PREP TIME: 5 minutes
TOTAL COOKING TIME: 6 to 8 hours

PERFECTLY EASY EVERYDAY BROWN RICE

▸ SOY-FREE ▸ GLUTEN-FREE

I typically use my rice cooker to make rice, but it's nice to have the slow cooker as an option. It's perfect for camping, or when you've run out of room on the stove. You can make half of this recipe, or store the leftovers in the fridge for eating later in the week.

INGREDIENTS:

2 cups (380 g) brown basmati rice, rinsed

4 cups (940 ml) water

Pinch of salt (optional)

DIRECTIONS:

Oil the crock of your slow cooker and add all the ingredients. Cook on high for 1 to 1½ hours. Check it after 45 minutes to make sure it's not cooking too quickly. It's important that you don't let the rice overcook, or it will turn to mush.

YIELD: 8 servings
TOTAL PREP TIME: 5 minutes
TOTAL COOKING TIME: 1 to 1½ hours

SERVING SUGGESTION

Leftover rice also freezes well. I like to have some extra on hand for making impromptu Apple Sage Sausage (page 23).

CHICKENY BOUILLON

▶ SOY-FREE ▶ GLUTEN-FREE*

Bouillon adds a bold flavor that you just can't get from using a plain vegetable broth.
Use this in soups, casseroles, and stews to elevate the dish to the next delicious level.
Freeze any leftovers, so you can have some on hand whenever you need it.

INGREDIENTS:

1 large onion, cut into quarters

2 medium-size carrots, chopped

2 sprigs fresh thyme or 1 teaspoon dried

2 stalks celery, chopped, or 4 sprigs lovage, including the stems, minced

2 sprigs fresh parsley or 1 teaspoon dried

½ cup (120 ml) water

½ teaspoon pepper (or to taste)

½ teaspoon salt (optional or to taste)

½ cup (48 g) nutritional yeast (*use gluten-free)

DID YOU KNOW?

Lovage is an herb whose stem and leaves have a strong celery taste. I use it in place of celery whenever I can. You can also substitute another herb called cutting celery. I find myself composting part of every bunch of celery I buy, so using lovage helps me curb food waste. You should be able to find either at your farmers' market. If not, try growing some yourself in a large container.

☾ THE NIGHT BEFORE:

Combine the cut-up vegetables and herbs in an airtight container and store them in the fridge.

☀ IN THE MORNING:

The water will keep the veggies from sticking to the crock, but you can spray the empty crock with oil before adding your ingredients for extra security. Combine the onion, carrots, thyme, celery, parsley, water, pepper, and salt to the slow cooker. Cook on low for 8 to 12 hours. You can cook this for as long as 12 hours and it will still come out great.

After cooking, remove the thyme sprigs. Add the contents of the crock and the nutritional yeast to a blender or food processor. You can also use an immersion blender if you want, but the texture won't be quite as smooth.

Refrigerate the amount you will use in a week. Put the rest in ice cube trays and freeze. Once the cubes are solid, remove them from the trays and put in a resealable freezer bag.

Use twice as much of this recipe as you would store-bought bouillon in your favorite recipes. For example, I typically use 1 to 2 tablespoons (6 to 12 g) of store-bought bouillon per recipe, so I use 2 to 4 tablespoons (12 to 24 g) of this recipe. (The average ice cube tray slot holds about 2 tablespoons [12 g], so this equals 1 or 2 ice cubes.)

YIELD: 1½ to 2 cups (144 to 192 g)
TOTAL PREP TIME: 10 minutes
TOTAL COOKING TIME: 8 to 12 hours

BEEFY BOUILLON

▶ SOY-FREE ▶ GLUTEN-FREE

This bouillon adds a dark, rich flavor to dishes. This recipe freezes great, so you can
have some on hand whenever you need it. Try adding it to sauces, soups, and stews.

INGREDIENTS:

½ cup (29 g) assorted dried mushrooms

1 large onion, cut into quarters

4 cloves garlic

1 cup (235 ml) water

¼ teaspoon soy sauce

RECIPE IDEAS & VARIATIONS

If you don't like onions, go ahead and leave them
out. Some people feel that they can overpower some
delicate soups.

A WORTHY NOTE

If mushrooms aren't processing properly, bake in
the oven at 350°F (180°C, or gas mark 4) for about
5 minutes and blend again.

☾ THE NIGHT BEFORE:

Process the mushrooms into a powder using a food processor or spice grinder. Combine the cut-up vegetables
in a covered container and store in the refrigerator.

☀ IN THE MORNING:

The water will keep the veggies from sticking to the crock,
but you can spray the empty crock with oil before adding
your ingredients for extra security. Add everything to the
slow cooker. Cook on low for 8 to 12 hours. As with the
Chickeny Bouillon (page 19), you don't need to worry
about coming home on time because you can cook this for
as long as 12 hours and it will still come out great.

Add the contents of the crock to a blender or food processor. Beware: If it's too full, the hot liquid might push the lid
off. You can also use an immersion blender if you want, but
the texture won't be as smooth.

Keep what you think you will use in a week and store it in
the fridge. Put the rest in ice cube trays and freeze. Once
the cubes are solid, remove them from the trays and put
in a resealable freezer bag.

Use twice as much of this recipe as you would store-
bought bouillon in your favorite recipes. I typically use
1 to 2 tablespoons (6 to 12 g) of store-bought per recipe,
so I use 2 to 4 tablespoons (12 to 24 g) of this recipe.
(The average ice cube tray slot holds about 2 tablespoons
[12 g], so this equals 1 or 2 ice cubes.)

YIELD: 1½ cups (144 g)
TOTAL PREP TIME: 10 minutes
TOTAL COOKING TIME: 8 to 12 hours

CHICK'N SEITAN

▶ SOY-FREE

I plan one day a month to make my own seitan. It takes less work than
you might think and you can control everything that goes into it.

....

FOR BROTH:

7 cups (1645 ml) water

2 cloves garlic, crushed

2 bay leaves

1 stalk celery, minced, or 2 sprigs lovage

1 sprig parsley

1½ tablespoons (9 g) vegan chicken-flavored bouillon
or 3 tablespoons (18 g) Chickeny Bouillon (page 19)

FOR THE SEITAN:

1½ cups (352 ml) water

1½ cups (150 g) vital wheat gluten

⅓ cup (32 g) nutritional yeast

1 tablespoon (16 g) tomato paste

¼ teaspoon salt

1 tablespoon (4.3 g) dried thyme (optional)

1 tablespoon (9 g) garlic powder (optional)

DIRECTIONS:

To make the broth: Combine all the broth ingredients in
your slow cooker and turn it on high. Your broth can heat
up while you make the seitan.

To make the seitan: In a large bowl, combine all of the
seitan ingredients. Mix until combined and knead for
5 minutes. (You can use a mixer with a dough hook, or
put it in a bread machine on the dough cycle for about
5 minutes.) Let the dough rest for about 5 minutes.

Stretch the dough out to the thickness you want and cut
into desired sizes. I usually do 4 chicken breast–size pieces
about the size of my palm and the rest in smaller chunks,
but you could make strips, nuggets, or medallions.

Drop the seitan pieces into the slow cooker. You'll know it's
done when the pieces float to the top, 2 to 3 hours. It may
look like they all stuck together, but once you take them
out of the broth they will easily come apart.

Store in the fridge submerged in the broth, or freeze extra
in the broth to use later. I try to freeze it in recipe-size portions, so I can defrost only the amount I need.

YIELD: 1¾ pounds (795 g)
TOTAL PREP TIME: 25 minutes
TOTAL COOKING TIME: 2 to 3 hours

SERVING SUGGESTIONS

Use the chicken breast-shaped pieces in Chick'n
Marsala (page 129), Chick'n Mushroom Casserole
(page 93), and Mix-and-Match Jambalaya (page 109).
Remember, you can make any shape you want. Try
making them nugget shaped, then bread them and
bake them in the oven for a perfect lunch box treat.

A WORTHY NOTE

This seitan is wetter than what you buy in the store.
It's made especially for cooking again in a slow
cooker recipe. It is not good for grilling, but it can be
used in other recipes that call for gluten.

BEEFY SEITAN

▶ SOY-FREE

This is great for the New Orleans Po' Boy (page 146), pepper steak, and other traditional beef recipes. Grate it for barbecue or use like you would ground meat. It freezes well, and you can use any leftover broth in other dishes.

FOR THE BROTH:

7 cups (1,645 ml) water

2 tablespoons (30 ml) soy sauce

2 sprigs fresh rosemary

FOR THE SEITAN:

1½ cups (352 ml) water

2 cups (240 g) vital wheat gluten

⅓ cup (32 g) nutritional yeast

1 tablespoon (16 g) tomato paste

½ teaspoon garlic powder

¼ teaspoon pepper

1 tablespoon (15 ml) soy sauce

2 tablespoons (30 g) ketchup

1 tablespoon (15 ml) vegan Worcestershire sauce

1 tablespoon (16 g) hoisin sauce

2 tablespoons (30 ml) Kitchen Bouquet
(optional, for color)

DID YOU KNOW?

Kitchen Bouquet is a product that's used to add color to gravies, and it works great on seitan as well.

DIRECTIONS:

To make the broth: Combine all the broth ingredients in your slow cooker and turn it on high. Your broth can heat up while you make the seitan.

To make the seitan: In a large bowl, combine all the seitan ingredients. Mix until combined and knead for 10 minutes. (You can use a mixer with the dough hook, or put it in a bread machine on the dough cycle for about 10 minutes.) Let the dough rest for about 5 minutes.

Stretch the dough out to the thickness you want and cut into desired sizes. I usually do 4 steak-size pieces (for the Hearty Faux Steak and Gravy recipe on page 126), cut some into strips, and roll the rest into a small roast to shred for sandwiches. You can shape into chunks, squares, or medallions if you want. If you make very large steak or roast pieces, you will need to turn them over with tongs, because their weight will make them sink to the bottom of the slow cooker, and they are not likely to float up. My first steaks got completely stuck to the bottom of the crock, but they moved easily once I grabbed them with tongs.

Drop the seitan pieces into the slow cooker. It's done when the pieces float to the top or if it's cooked for the full 3 hours. It may look like they are all stuck together, but once you take them out of the broth they will easily come apart.

Store in the fridge submerged in the broth or freeze extra in the broth to use later. I try to freeze it in recipe-size portion, so I can thaw the exact amount I need.

YIELD: 1⅔ pounds (754 g)
TOTAL PREP TIME: 25 minutes
TOTAL COOKING TIME: 2 to 3 hours

APPLE SAGE SAUSAGE

▶ SOY-FREE ▶ GLUTEN-FREE*

This is a great way to make your own vegan sausage to use in other recipes. The texture is similar to Gimme Lean. You can cook it in the slow cooker in one large piece and crumble it in a food processor, or make patties with the uncooked mixture, and then cook on the stove top or in the oven. The crumbles and the cooked patties freeze great, so make a batch once a month.

INGREDIENTS:

1½ cups (248 g) cooked brown rice

1 cup (110 g) walnuts pieces

1 cup (120 g) vital wheat gluten

2 tablespoons (12 g) nutritional yeast

1 cup (250 g) applesauce

2 tablespoons (14 g) ground flaxseed mixed with 2 tablespoons (30 ml) warm water

1 tablespoon (6 g) vegan chicken-flavored bouillon or 2 tablespoons (12 g) Chickeny Bouillon (page 19)

2 tablespoons (4 g) sage

1 teaspoon thyme

1 teaspoon oregano

1 teaspoon Hungarian paprika

½ to 1 teaspoon salt (to taste, use less if your bouillon is salty)

Pepper, to taste

☾ THE NIGHT BEFORE:

In a food processor, pulse the walnuts and cooked rice until the mixture is coarsely ground but not puréed. Combine the nut mixture with the remaining ingredients in a large mixing bowl. Cover and refrigerate.

☀ IN THE MORNING:

Put the mixture into an oiled slow cooker crock. Cook on high for 1½ to 2 hours.

Break the loaf down into small pieces in the food processor, and process until it crumbles. Store what you won't use in a week in the freezer. I use quart-size freezer bags.

YIELD: 6 to 8 servings
TOTAL PREP TIME: 10 minutes
TOTAL COOKING TIME: 1½ to 2 hours

SERVING SUGGESTIONS

This is great in the From-the-Pantry Pot Pie (page 88), the Meatless Sausage and Mushroom Ragu (page 103), or in any recipe with sausage crumbles.

*GLUTEN-FREE VERSION

Make this gluten-free by changing three things in the recipe. Leave out the vital wheat gluten and use 1½ cups (165 g) walnuts and 2 cups (330 g) brown rice instead of the amounts listed. Instead of using the slow cooker, oil a baking sheet and form the mixture into patties. Bake in a 350°F (180°C or gas mark 4) oven for about 15 minutes, then turn them over and cook for 10 to 15 more minutes. Do not try to cook the gluten-free version in the slow cooker.

TEA-SCENTED TOFU

▶ GLUTEN-FREE

Here is an easy way to make a uniquely flavored tofu. It's becoming harder to find smoked tofu in the stores, so I use smoked tea when I cook mine. You can use your favorite marinades to design your own bold flavors. I like to use lapsang souchong tea, which is a smoked tea, but you can use blackberry, jasmine, or any flavored tea you have on hand.

....

INGREDIENTS:

1 package (15 ounces, or 420 g) firm tofu

FOR THE SMOKING INGREDIENTS:

4 tablespoons (14 g) loose black tea

4 tablespoons (12 g) raw rice

4 tablespoons (60 g) brown sugar

RECIPE IDEAS & VARIATIONS

Try adding other flavors to the smoking mixture, such as anise, citrus zest, chiles, or cinnamon sticks. Get adventurous and smoke tempeh, seitan, and mushrooms to add a punch of flavor to your favorite dishes.

A WORTHY NOTE

Don't have any loose tea on hand? Tear open tea bags and use the tea in those instead.

DIRECTIONS:

Drain the tofu, and cut the block in half widthwise. Now cut each half into 3 pieces for a total of 6 pieces. Take a clean dish towel and place 2 of the tofu pieces side by side and roll the towel over. Now add 2 more on top of that and roll the towel again. Repeat one more time, and place on a flat surface. Take a large pan and put something heavy in it such as a bag of flour or rice. Place this on top of the rolled-up tofu to press the water out. Let sit for 10 to 15 minutes, then unroll and use.

Use aluminum foil to cover your slow cooker, so the sugar doesn't burn on the crock and ruin it. I tear 2 long pieces of foil and arrange it like a cross inside the crock, so the 2 pieces overlap. This completely covers a round crock. You may need to add 2 more pieces to cover a large oval crock.

To make the smoking ingredients: Spread the tea, rice, and brown sugar on top of the foil. Now put a vegetable steamer basket (metal or silicone) into the crock over the smoking ingredients. Place the tofu slices on the steamer in a single layer, if possible.

Cook on high for at least 2 hours, then cook on low for 6 to 10 more hours. Turn the tofu over about halfway through. The longer you cook the tofu, the denser it will be. You can keep cooking it until it's almost a jerky consistency, so check it after 8 hours to decide whether you want to cook it longer. Store in the fridge for up to a week or freeze for up to 2 months.

YIELD: 6 servings
TOTAL PREP TIME: 15 minutes
TOTAL COOKING TIME: 8 to 12 hours

PRESERVE-THE-HARVEST DICED TOMATOES

▸ SOY-FREE ▸ GLUTEN-FREE

Here's an easy, free-form recipe. Give it a try and you'll get that satisfied feeling when you use your handiwork in soups and stews later in the year. Try to cook the tomatoes on the same day you buy or pick them, if possible.

INGREDIENTS:
Tomatoes to fill your crock

A WORTHY NOTE

At the farmers' market, select tomatoes that are not overripe or mushy. I try to buy up all the imperfect tomatoes at my market. They are sometimes called "ugly," "seconds," or another creative word to let you know why they cost less per pound than the perfect tomatoes. Many times you can buy these at one-third of the perfect tomato price, making it even more of a bargain.

I do not peel the tomatoes, because I always use organic or at least pesticide-free ones. But if yours aren't organic you can drop them in boiling water for a couple of minutes after making a small X in the bottom of each with a knife. Once they're cool enough to handle, the skins will slide right off. Dice and proceed as indicated.

DIRECTIONS:

Rinse the tomatoes. Take the whole tomatoes, and put them in your crock one at a time until they peek out over the rim. This is how many tomatoes you can cook in your slow cooker. Remove the tomatoes, and now you will prep them for cooking.

Peeled or not, dice the tomatoes. Be sure to remove the top of the stem and any bruised or mushy parts. Put the diced tomatoes and their juice in the slow cooker. Cook on low for 6 to 8 hours, or on high for about 3 hours.

Make sure the tomatoes are completely cool before freezing them. Many times I cool them in the fridge overnight before I pack them.

You can use a freezer-safe container or a resealable plastic bag that says it's for the freezer. Those bags are thicker and help their contents to stay fresh longer. The bags are easy to stack in the smallest freezer. I put about $1\frac{1}{2}$ cups (270 g, about the size of 1 can of tomatoes) per bag, carefully push the air out, and close. Wipe off the outside of the bag to make sure it's dry, or they will freeze together. Stack them on top of one another, so they will freeze in that thinner shape.

Pull a bag out the night before you need it and thaw it in the fridge. Or, because the bag and its contents were frozen thin, run cold water over the bag in the sink. Most of all, enjoy not going out to the store to buy a can of tomatoes in the middle of a snowstorm!

YIELD: Depends on the size of your slow cooker and how many tomatoes it holds
TOTAL PREP TIME: 20 minutes
TOTAL COOKING TIME: 6 to 8 hours on low or about 3 hours on high

BEYOND-EASY BAKED POTATOES

▶ SOY-FREE   ▶ GLUTEN-FREE

This is the perfect no-fuss meal. Cook them the night before and pack one for lunch, or throw them in the slow cooker in the morning and have them for dinner.

It's true that you use no water in the slow cooker for this recipe, and no oil is needed to coat the potato. It really is as easy as it seems. You can also cook 1 or 2 potatoes in a 1- to 1½-quart (940 ml to 1.4 L) slow cooker.

INGREDIENTS:

4 large russet potatoes (use organic so you can eat the skin), washed and scrubbed

RECIPE IDEAS & VARIATIONS

- Bake the potatoes, then mash them for the perfect side to any dish. Just put into a bowl, and mash with nondairy milk and nondairy butter. Super simple!

- Try cooking some sweet potatoes using the same method. Serve topped with a little brown sugar and cinnamon for a surprise dessert.

- Top with leftover stew or beans to make a hearty meal.

DIRECTIONS:

Make a few holes in each potato with a fork. Put them in the slow cooker.

Cook on low for 6 to 8 hours. Enjoy your perfectly baked potato.

YIELD: 4 servings
TOTAL PREP TIME: 3 minutes
TOTAL COOKING TIME: 6 to 8 hours

ALL-OCCASION ROASTED GARLIC

▸ SOY-FREE ▸ GLUTEN-FREE

This is a great no-fuss treat that's good for you and your waistline. Once it's cooked, just squeeze the cloves, or use a knife to get them out from the skins. It's true you use no water. It really is as easy as it seems.

INGREDIENTS:
4 to 6 heads garlic

DIRECTIONS:
Cut off the top of each garlic head (the pointy side) to expose the cloves. Place in the slow cooker cut side up. Cook on low for 3 to 4 hours. Let cool completely before squeezing the cloves from the skins. Store in the fridge for up to a week.

YIELD: 4 to 6 heads garlic
TOTAL PREP TIME: 1 minute
TOTAL COOKING TIME: 3 to 4 hours

RECIPE IDEAS & VARIATIONS

You can also cook 1 or 2 heads of garlic in a 1 to 1½-quart (940 ml to 1.4 L) slow cooker.

SERVING SUGGESTION

Spread on bread instead of olive oil or nondairy butter; use on pizza and in pastas.

CITRUS RUM BBQ SAUCE

▶ SOY-FREE ▶ GLUTEN-FREE

Tired of having to read labels with words on them that have little or nothing to do with food? Make your own barbecue sauce at home. This one is slightly sweet from the rum and orange juice, and seasoned with thyme, allspice, and ginger. It makes a mean barbecue tempeh or tofu sandwich. Freeze the leftovers in ice cube trays, and defrost a cube or two the next time you crave a sandwich.

INGREDIENTS:

2 tablespoons (30 ml) olive oil

1 onion, minced

2 cloves garlic, minced

1 teaspoon grated ginger

1 can (14½ ounces, or 406 g) tomato sauce

1 can (6 ounces, or 170 g) tomato paste

½ cup (120 ml) orange juice

½ lime, juiced

½ cup (120 ml) rum (amber or dark, if possible)

2 tablespoons (30 ml) apple cider vinegar

2 tablespoons (30 ml) agave nectar or maple syrup

3 tablespoons (45 g) brown sugar

1 teaspoon dried thyme

½ teaspoon allspice

½ teaspoon paprika

Pinch of ground cloves

☾ THE NIGHT BEFORE:

Heat the oil in a skillet over medium heat, add the onion, and cook until translucent, 3 to 5 minutes. Add the garlic and cook for about 1 minute more. Transfer to an airtight container and store in the fridge overnight.

☼ IN THE MORNING:

Combine all the ingredients in the slow cooker. Cook on low for 8 to 10 hours. If the sauce is still too thin, turn the slow cooker to high and prop the lid up with the handle of a wooden spoon. This will allow some of the liquid to evaporate. Only keep the amount of sauce you will use in a week in the fridge. Store the rest in the freezer for up to 6 months.

YIELD: 3 to 4 cups (750 to 1,000 g)
TOTAL PREP TIME: 10 minutes
TOTAL COOKING TIME: 8 to 10 hours

SERVING SUGGESTION

After the sauce has been cooked, add shredded seitan or tofu. Cook on low for 6 to 8 hours. Serve on toasted buns.

BALSAMIC ONION MARMALADE

▸ SOY-FREE ▸ GLUTEN-FREE

This is not the marmalade to spread on your morning toast, but the sweetness of the cooked onions contrasts nicely with the balsamic vinegar. Use on crostini, on top of pizza, or anywhere else you think it will be appreciated.

INGREDIENTS:

4 large onions

½ cup (120 ml) water

¼ cup (60 ml) balsamic vinegar

2 tablespoons (30 ml) olive oil

2 tablespoons (25 to 30 g) sugar, agave nectar, or maple syrup

1 sprig fresh rosemary

½ to 1 teaspoon salt (to taste)

☾ THE NIGHT BEFORE:

Slice the onions and store in an airtight container in the fridge.

☀ IN THE MORNING:

Add all the ingredients to the slow cooker. Cook on low for 6 to 8 hours. Remove and discard the rosemary sprig. Let cool completely before using or storing. Store in the fridge for up to a week or freeze for up to 2 months.

YIELD: 2 to 3 cups (500 to 750 g)
TOTAL PREP TIME: 5 minutes
TOTAL COOKING TIME: 6 to 8 hours

SERVING SUGGESTIONS

Use on pizzas, in pastas, or on hot dogs or veggie burgers. The marmalade can also be used to top bruschetta or on top of spreads such as hummus.

HOMEMADE SMOKY KETCHUP

▸ SOY-FREE ▸ GLUTEN-FREE

Most people love ketchup and always have it on hand. Try making your own. It's really easy in the slow cooker because it cooks while you're away. This recipe has a smoky flavor, but you can make your own signature ketchup by omitting some or all of the spices in the recipe and adding curry powder or roasted garlic instead. You are only as limited as your imagination.

INGREDIENTS:

2 tablespoons (30 ml) olive oil

$\frac{1}{2}$ small onion, minced

2 cloves garlic, minced

1 can (20 ounces, or 560 g) crushed tomatoes (fire-roasted, if possible), drained

2 tablespoons (32 g) tomato paste

$\frac{1}{2}$ cup (115 g) packed brown sugar

$\frac{1}{2}$ cup (120 ml) apple cider vinegar (you can use white or rice vinegar instead)

$\frac{1}{2}$ teaspoon salt (to taste)

$\frac{1}{4}$ teaspoon chipotle chile powder

$\frac{1}{4}$ teaspoon allspice

$\frac{1}{4}$ teaspoon celery seed

$\frac{1}{8}$ teaspoon dry mustard

$\frac{1}{8}$ teaspoon ground cloves

$\frac{1}{8}$ teaspoon ground ginger

☾ THE NIGHT BEFORE:

Heat the oil in a skillet over medium heat, add the onion, and cook until translucent, 3 to 5 minutes. Add the garlic and cook for about 1 minute more. Transfer to an airtight container and store in the fridge overnight.

☼ IN THE MORNING:

Combine all the ingredients in the slow cooker. Cook on low for 8 to 10 hours. If the ketchup is still too thin, turn the slow cooker to high and prop the lid up with the handle of a wooden spoon. This will allow some of the liquid to evaporate.

YIELD: 2 to $2\frac{1}{2}$ cups (500 to 625 g)
TOTAL PREP TIME: 10 minutes
TOTAL COOKING TIME: 8 to 10 hours

A WORTHY NOTE

- Only keep the amount of ketchup you will use in a week in the fridge. Store the rest in the freezer for up to 6 months.

- You can use Preserve-the-Harvest Diced Tomatoes (page 25) instead of canned crushed tomatoes. Just purée them first, or purée the batch of ketchup after cooking.

FALL HARVEST FRUIT BUTTER

▸ SOY-FREE ▸ GLUTEN-FREE

Serve up a bit of fall all winter long by freezing some of this recipe.
It's perfect on toast, English muffins, or bagels. The spices scent your house
while it's cooking, which is a bonus. This is my friend Faith's favorite recipe.

INGREDIENTS:

6 large pears, peeled, cored, and chopped

4 large apples (or about 6 medium ones), peeled, cored, and chopped

2 cups (300 g) cubed fresh pumpkin or butternut squash

Juice of 2 lemons

1/2 cup (115 g) packed brown sugar (you can substitute 1/2 cup [120 ml] agave nectar or maple syrup)

1 teaspoon cinnamon

1/2 teaspoon allspice

1/2 teaspoon cardamom

1/2 teaspoon ground ginger

1/4 teaspoon ground cloves

DIRECTIONS:

Oil the crock of your slow cooker. Combine all the ingredients in the slow cooker. Prop the lid open by placing the thin edge of a wooden spoon handle lengthwise across the crock. This will allow the liquid to evaporate. Cook on low for 8 to 10 hours, until most of the liquid has evaporated.

If you need to evaporate more liquid, switch the slow cooker to high, leave the lid propped up, and cook for 1 to 2 hours longer.

Purée the mixture in batches using an immersion blender or a countertop blender. Let cool completely.

Transfer to freezer bags or special freezer containers for preserves. Store in the freezer for 3 to 4 months.

YIELD: 6 to 8 cups (1,920 to 2,560 g)
TOTAL PREP TIME: 20 minutes
TOTAL COOKING TIME: 8 to 10 hours

SERVING SUGGESTION

Want to make a fast and fancy dessert? Combine about 1 cup (320 g) of the fruit butter with 1 container (12 ounces, 336 g) silken tofu in a food processor. Blend until very smooth, stopping periodically to scrape down the sides. Serve chilled in martini glasses as a mousse, or put in a graham cracker crust for a super easy Thanksgiving pie.

A WORTHY NOTE

No fresh pumpkin on hand? Use 1 can (15 ounces, or 420 g) pumpkin purée or 2 cups (490 g) Perfect Pumpkin Purée (page 34).

PERFECT PUMPKIN PURÉE

▸ SOY-FREE ▸ GLUTEN-FREE

Never worry about a canned pumpkin shortage again. Each fall, pie pumpkins
are sprinkled in with the larger jack-o'-lantern pumpkins. Pie pumpkins
are smaller and many will even fit in a 1½-quart (1.4 L) slow cooker.

INGREDIENTS:

1 pie pumpkin that will fit in your slow cooker

A WORTHY NOTE

• Use in any recipe that calls for cooked or canned
  pumpkin in the same portion as called for.

• Freeze in 1½-cup (368 g) portions, so you can
  thaw the same amount that's in one 12-ounce
  (368 g) can.

DIRECTIONS:

Wash the pumpkin, and poke holes in it for the steam to
escape. Place it in the slow cooker and cook on low for 6 to
8 hours. When it's ready, a fork should easily slide through
the skin and the flesh.

Let the pumpkin cool until you can touch it without burning yourself. Move it to a cutting board, and slice it in half.
Remove the seeds and pumpkin guts. Scrape the flesh into
a food processor or blender and purée until smooth.

YIELD: 3 to 6 cups (735 to 1,470 g)
TOTAL PREP TIME: 3 minutes
TOTAL COOKING TIME: 6 to 8 hours

DID YOU KNOW?

Pie pumpkins are tastier and meant to be used in
cooking because they are fleshier.

BRANDIED CRANBERRY SAUCE

▸ SOY-FREE ▸ GLUTEN-FREE

This sophisticated version of a holiday favorite is amazingly easy to make.
This recipe requires a small 1- or 1½-quart (940 ml or 1.4 L) slow cooker.

INGREDIENTS:

1 bag (12 ounces, or 340 g) fresh cranberries

½ cup (120 ml) orange juice

½ cup (120 ml) agave nectar or maple syrup

¼ cup (63 ml) brandy

DIRECTIONS:

Oil the crock of your slow cooker. Add all the ingredients to the slow cooker. Cook on high for 2½ to 3½ hours. After the first hour prop the lid up on the handle of a wooden spoon to allow the sauce to reduce.

YIELD: 1½ to 2 cups (375 to 500 g)
TOTAL PREP TIME: 5 minutes
TOTAL COOKING TIME: 2½ to 3½ hours

SERVING SUGGESTION

Use leftovers to top your morning oatmeal, or purée with silken tofu to make a cranberry pudding.

RECIPE IDEAS & VARIATIONS

You can double or triple the recipe and use a larger slow cooker if you like.

CHAPTER 3

SIMMERING SOUPS THAT COOK WHILE YOU'RE AWAY

Soups are one of the best things to make in a slow cooker, and most of these soups can cook even longer than their stated times, so if you end up coming home really late from work, your dinner won't be ruined. Still, be sure to add a little extra liquid if your slow cooker runs hot or you know you will be more than an hour or two late just to be on the safe side.

In many of the recipes I do ask that you sauté onions and sometimes garlic before you add them to your soups and stews. You can easily do this the night before when you are cleaning up from that night's dinner, and you'll have them waiting in the fridge to use the next day. It really makes the whole dish taste better. If you are in a hurry, or forget to cook them the night before, go ahead and add them raw if you are going to cook it for at least 8 hours.

Another thing to note is that you will need to taste the soup and add extra salt, pepper, herbs, or spices before serving. One person will like more seasoning than another, and the long cooking process can dull the flavor of some herbs and spices.

1. Golden Borscht
2. Herbed Carrot and Baby Turnip Soup
3. Creamy Corn Chowder
4. Summer Squash Bisque
5. Asparagus Tarragon Soup
6. Spring Minestrone with Pesto Parmesan
7. Sweet Potato White Bean Soup
8. Cauliflower and Celery Root Bisque
9. Thai Coconut Pumpkin Soup
10. Hungarian Mushroom Soup
11. Asian Tofu Soup
12. Tortilla Soup
13. Hot and Sour Soup
14. Split Pea and Apple Soup
15. Delicata Squash and Pear Soup
16. Turbodog Root Veggie Soup
17. Split Pea and Lentil Soup
18. Smoked Tofu and Stars Soup
19. What's in the Freezer? Veggie Soup
20. Creamy Potato Soup
21. Citrus Black Bean Soup

GOLDEN BORSCHT

▸ SOY-FREE ▸ GLUTEN-FREE

I don't understand the beets-taste-like-dirt people, and I even live with one. Earthy and dirt just aren't the same thing to me. A good way to sneak them in is to use yellow beets. If the beets aren't red, most people don't notice them and tend to be more open-minded. In this soup, the beets and potatoes are almost the same color after cooking. Feel free to call it golden veggie soup in case your dinner companions know borscht has beets in it!

INGREDIENTS:

3 large yellow beets (about 1½ pounds, or 680 g), peeled and chopped

2 medium-size carrots, cut into half-moons

2 cups (180 g) chopped cabbage

2 cloves garlic, minced

2 fist-size potatoes, peeled if not organic and diced

6 cups (1410 ml) water

2 tablespoons (12 g) vegan chicken-flavored bouillon or 4 tablespoons (24 g) Chickeny Bouillon (page 19)

4 teaspoons (21 g) tomato paste

1 bay leaf

1 large sprig fresh thyme or 1 teaspoon dried

1 teaspoon dried dill

1 teaspoon agave nectar or maple syrup

1 to 2 tablespoons (15 to 30 ml) apple cider vinegar or lemon juice (to taste)

1 teaspoon pepper (or to taste)

½ teaspoon salt (or to taste)

Vegan sour cream or Cashew Sour Cream (page 47), for serving (optional)

Fresh dill, for serving (optional)

☾ THE NIGHT BEFORE:

Store the cut-up vegetables in an airtight container in the fridge.

☼ IN THE MORNING:

Combine the cut-up vegetables, water, bouillon, tomato paste, bay leaf, and thyme to the slow cooker. Cook on low for 6 to 8 hours.

Remove and discard the thyme sprig. Add the dill, agave nectar, and apple cider vinegar, and adjust the seasonings to make the sweet-sour ratio to your liking. Add the salt and pepper to taste.

Top the bowls of hot soup with a dollop of sour cream and a sprig of fresh dill.

YIELD: 6 servings
TOTAL PREP TIME: 20 minutes
TOTAL COOKING TIME: 6 to 8 hours

RECIPE IDEAS & VARIATIONS

You can use any color beets in this recipe if you have trouble finding yellow ones.

HERBED CARROT AND BABY TURNIP SOUP

▸ SOY-FREE ▸ GLUTEN-FREE

Turnips may not be your favorite veggie, but if you've never had baby turnips you should definitely give them another try. The flavor is delicate, and they are great steamed on their own, too.

INGREDIENTS:

2 pounds (908 g) carrots, tops removed, cut into large chunks

6 baby turnips, tops removed, cut into quarters

6 cups (1,410 ml) water

2 tablespoons (12 g) vegan chicken-flavored bouillon or 4 tablespoons (24 g) Chickeny Bouillon (page 19)

2 sprigs fresh rosemary

5 sprigs fresh thyme, plus extra for garnish

Salt and pepper, to taste

☾ THE NIGHT BEFORE:

Store the cut-up vegetables in an airtight container in the fridge.

☀ IN THE MORNING:

Combine all the ingredients in the slow cooker. Cook on low for 6 to 8 hours.

Remove and discard the rosemary sprig. Purée in batches in a food process or blender, being careful of splatters from the hot soup, adjust the seasonings, and serve. Chop the extra thyme for garnish and sprinkle on top.

YIELD: 6 servings
TOTAL PREP TIME: 10 minutes
TOTAL COOKING TIME: 6 to 8 hours

RECIPE IDEAS & VARIATIONS

You can use larger turnips in this soup. Just make sure to peel them if they are not baby ones.

DID YOU KNOW?

Turnips are high in fiber, vitamin C, calcium, and potassium.

CREAMY CORN CHOWDER

▶ SOY-FREE ▶ GLUTEN-FREE

Corn chowder is a great summer soup because of the abundant fresh corn and basil. But it works in winter, too, if you keep some frozen corn and basil on hand. Once some of the soup is puréed and the nondairy milk is added, it creates a creamy base studded with veggies and herbs.

....

INGREDIENTS:

1 pound (454 g) potatoes, peeled if not organic and chopped

1 bell pepper, chopped

4 cloves garlic, minced

1 pound (454 g) fresh or frozen corn kernels

4 cups (940 ml) water

3 tablespoons (18 g) vegan chicken-flavored bouillon or 6 tablespoons (36 g) Chickeny Bouillon (page 19)

4 sprigs fresh thyme or 2 teaspoons dried

2 tablespoons chopped fresh basil, plus extra for garnish

2 cups (470 ml) nondairy milk

Salt and pepper, to taste

Shredded vegan cheddar cheese, for serving

Vegan sour cream or Cashew Sour Cream (page 47), for serving

☾ THE NIGHT BEFORE:

Store the cut-up vegetables in an airtight container in the fridge.

☀ IN THE MORNING:

Combine the potatoes, pepper, garlic, corn, water, bouillon, and thyme in the slow cooker. Cook on low for 6 to 8 hours.

About 30 minutes before serving, remove and discard the thyme sprigs and carefully transfer 2 cups (470 ml) of the hot soup to a blender or food processor and purée. Return purée to the slow cooker to thicken the soup. Add the basil and nondairy milk. Turn the slow cooker up to high. Cook for about 30 minutes, until the soup is very hot. Add salt and pepper to taste.

Top bowls of hot soup with the cheese, sour cream, and extra fresh basil.

YIELD: 6 servings
TOTAL PREP TIME: 15 minutes
TOTAL COOKING TIME: 6 to 8 hours

DID YOU KNOW?

Buy (or grow) extra basil in the summer when it is plentiful. Purée it with a little olive oil, and freeze in ice cube trays. Once the cubes are frozen solid, pop them out into a resealable freezer bag. In the winter you can add a few cubes of basil to soups and stews.

SUMMER SQUASH BISQUE

▶ SOY-FREE ▶ GLUTEN-FREE

This is a light, creamy soup with a hint of lemon from the lemon basil. It's perfect for summer when squash and basil are cheap and plentiful. You can use nondairy milk instead of the creamer if you want to cut down on the fat content.

INGREDIENTS:

4 cups (480 g) chopped assorted summer squash

2 cloves garlic, minced

3 cups (705 ml) water

2 tablespoons (12 g) vegan chicken-flavored bouillon or 4 tablespoons (24 g) Chickeny Bouillon (page 19)

1 teaspoon salt

Pepper, to taste

¼ cup (60 ml) plain coconut creamer or other nondairy creamer

10 leaves fresh lemon basil or other variety basil plus juice of ½ lemon

☪ THE NIGHT BEFORE:

Store the cut-up squash and garlic in an airtight container in the fridge.

☀ IN THE MORNING:

Combine the squash, garlic, water, bouillon, salt, and pepper in the slow cooker. Cook on low for 6 to 8 hours

Add the creamer and whole basil leaves and stir to combine. Purée the soup with an immersion blender or in batches in a countertop blender, being careful of splatters of hot soup, until smooth. Adjust the seasonings to taste.

YIELD: 6 servings
TOTAL PREP TIME: 10 minutes
TOTAL COOKING TIME: 6 to 8 hours

A WORTHY NOTE

You might not think about using your slow cooker in the summer, but it's a perfect way to keep your house cool. It puts off very little heat compared to the stove or oven.

ASPARAGUS TARRAGON SOUP

▶ SOY-FREE ▶ GLUTEN-FREE

Asparagus is the first veggie of the year to burst out of the dirt.
And it tastes brilliant in almost everything, too! This is a delicious,
soothing soup. It's the perfect way to celebrate the asparagus harvest.

INGREDIENTS:

2 bunches (about 2 pounds, or 908 g) asparagus

2 cups (470 ml) water

2 tablespoons (12 g) vegan chicken-flavored bouillon
or 4 tablespoons (24 g) Chickeny Bouillon (page 19)

1 tablespoon (4 g) fresh tarragon or 1 teaspoon dried

1 tablespoon (4 g) fresh marjoram or 1 teaspoon dried

1/2 to 1 cup (120 to 235 ml) nondairy creamer or milk
(unsweetened, if possible)

Salt and pepper, to taste

☾ THE NIGHT BEFORE:

Wash the asparagus and snap off the woody end of each
stalk and discard. Snap the stalks into 1-inch (2.5 cm)
pieces. Store in an airtight container in the refrigerator.

☀ IN THE MORNING:

Combine the asparagus, water, bouillon, tarragon, and
marjoram in the slow cooker. Cook on high for 1 1/2 to 2
hours, until the asparagus is completely cooked. Add
the creamer and stir to combine. Purée the soup with an
immersion blender or in batches in a countertop blender,
being careful of splatters of hot soup, until smooth. Add
salt and pepper to taste.

YIELD: 4 servings
TOTAL PREP TIME: 10 minutes
TOTAL COOKING TIME: 1 1/2 to 2 hours

A WORTHY NOTE

You can substitute frozen asparagus for fresh. Thaw
it the night before in the fridge, or increase the cooking time by 30 minutes to 1 hour.

SPRING MINESTRONE WITH PESTO PARMESAN

▸ SOY-FREE* ▸ GLUTEN-FREE*

Minestrone is a great soup anytime of the year. Serve with
focaccia and a big green salad for a complete meal.

....

FOR THE PESTO PARMESAN:

15 leaves fresh basil

2 sprigs fresh oregano

¼ cup (36 g) almonds

1 tablespoon (15 ml) olive oil (optional)

Salt, to taste

FOR THE MINESTRONE:

1 tablespoon (15 ml) olive oil

½ large onion, chopped

2 cloves garlic, minced

1-inch (2.5 cm) piece lemon peel

1 large carrot, chopped

1 yellow squash, cut into half-moons

1 bunch Swiss chard or beet greens, torn into small pieces

5 cups (1175 ml) water

2 tablespoons (12 g) vegan chicken-flavored bouillon
or 4 tablespoons (24 g) Chickeny Bouillon (page 19)

1 can (14½ ounces, or 406 g) white beans or chickpeas,
drained and rinsed

1 can (14½ ounces, or 406 g) diced tomatoes

2 vegan Italian sausages, chopped (*omit to make
gluten- and soy-free)

2-inch (5 cm) sprig fresh rosemary

Salt and pepper, to taste
Croutons, for serving

☾ THE NIGHT BEFORE:

To make the Parmesan: Put all the ingredients into a food
processor and pulse until it begins to form a grainy paste,
but is not smooth. You want the texture to be granular like
the grated Parmesan that you buy in a shaker. Store in an
airtight container in the fridge.

To make the minestrone: Heat the oil in a skillet over
medium heat and sauté the onion until translucent, 3 to
5 minutes. Add the garlic and sauté for 1 minute longer.
Combine the sautéed onion, lemon peel, and cut-up
vegetables in a large airtight container and store in the
refrigerator.

☼ IN THE MORNING:

Combine all the minestrone ingredients in the slow cooker.
Cook on low for 6 to 8 hours. Remove and discard the
rosemary sprig. Top bowls of hot soup with the Pesto
Parmesan and croutons.

YIELD: 6 servings
TOTAL PREP TIME: 15 minutes
TOTAL COOKING TIME: 6 to 8 hours

A WORTHY NOTE
You have to be careful when you are looking for
vegan sausages. There are a ton of veggie sausages
on the market, but many have eggs or dairy in them.
Be sure to read the ingredients carefully, especially if
you are trying a new one.

SWEET POTATO WHITE BEAN SOUP

▸ SOY-FREE ▸ GLUTEN-FREE

This soup packs tons of nutrients in a tasty package. It's a nice start to a larger meal, or serve it with a salad for a light dinner. The sweetness of the sweet potato hides the slight bitterness of the greens, so it's a great way to get your family to eat more greens.

INGREDIENTS:

1 medium-size sweet potato, chopped

2 cloves garlic, minced

2 stalks celery, chopped, or 2 sprigs lovage, minced

1 can (14½ ounces, or 406 g) diced tomatoes or 1½ cups (340 g) Preserve-the-Harvest Diced Tomatoes (page 25)

1 can (14½ ounces, or 406 g) white beans, drained and rinsed, or 1½ cups (340 g) homemade (page 17)

5 cups (1175 ml) water

2 tablespoons (12 g) vegan chicken-flavored bouillon or 4 tablespoons (24 g) Chickeny Bouillon (page 19)

2 cups (134 g) chopped Swiss chard

1 tablespoon (2.4 g) minced fresh thyme

2 sprigs parsley, minced

Salt and pepper, to taste

☾ THE NIGHT BEFORE:

Store the cut-up vegetables in separate airtight containers in the fridge.

☀ IN THE MORNING:

Combine the sweet potato, garlic, celery, diced tomatoes, beans, water, and bouillon in the slow cooker. Cook on low for 6 to 8 hours.

About 20 minutes before serving, add the Swiss chard, thyme, and parsley. Cook until the Swiss chard is tender. Add salt and pepper to taste.

YIELD: 6 servings
TOTAL PREP TIME: 15 minutes
TOTAL COOKING TIME: 6 to 8 hours

DID YOU KNOW?

Swiss chard has lots of vitamin A, C, and K and is also a good source of potassium.

CAULIFLOWER AND CELERY ROOT BISQUE

▸ SOY-FREE   ▸ GLUTEN-FREE

This recipe was inspired by the Cauliflower Bisque from Anna Thomas's book *Love Soup*.
Her earlier books opened my mind to exactly how much I could accomplish in my very own kitchen.
This soup is tangy from the lemon juice and super creamy and thick from the puréed celery root
and cauliflower. It's one of my favorite soups and is great topped with a few croutons.

INGREDIENTS:

1 thick slice lemon zest about 1 inch (2.5 cm) long

1 medium-size celery root, peeped and chopped

1 medium-size parsnip, peeped and chopped

4 cloves garlic, minced

30 ounces (840 g) fresh or frozen cauliflower,
    cut into florets

4 cups (940 ml) water

2 tablespoons (12 g) vegan chicken-flavored bouillon
    or 4 tablespoons (24 g) Chickeny Bouillon (page 19)

Juice of ½ lemon

1 tablespoon (7 g) herbes de Provence

Salt and pepper, to taste

☾ THE NIGHT BEFORE:

Store the cut-up vegetables in an airtight container in
the fridge.

If you are using frozen cauliflower, you do not need to
defrost it.

☀ IN THE MORNING:

Combine all the ingredients in the slow cooker. Cook on
low for 6 to 8 hours. Fish out the strip of lemon peel, then
purée the soup with an immersion blender or in small
batches in a countertop blender, being careful of splatters
of hot soup, until smooth. Adjust the seasonings to taste.

YIELD: 6 servings
TOTAL PREP TIME: 10 minutes
TOTAL COOKING TIME: 6 to 8 hours

SERVING SUGGESTION

One of my amazing recipe testers used leftover
bisque as a substitute for gravy over biscuits.

THAI COCONUT PUMPKIN SOUP

▶ SOY-FREE ▶ GLUTEN-FREE

This tasty recipe has lots of nutrition packaged into a rich, creamy, slightly spicy soup.

INGREDIENTS:

1 small pie pumpkin, peeled, seeded, and chopped
(about 2½ pounds, or 1135 g)

2 cloves garlic, minced

1½ tablespoons (12 g) peeled and grated ginger

1 stalk lemongrass, cut in half and bruised with a knife

2 cups (470 ml) water

2 tablespoons (12 g) vegan chicken-flavored bouillon
or 4 tablespoons (24 g) Chickeny Bouillon (page 19)

1 tablespoon (15 ml) agave nectar or maple syrup

½ teaspoon turmeric

½ teaspoon cumin

½ teaspoon coriander

½ teaspoon salt

¼ teaspoon chili powder

1 can (14 ounces, or 392 g) light coconut milk

Zest of ½ lime

☾ **THE NIGHT BEFORE:**

Store the cut-up vegetables in an airtight container in the fridge.

☼ **IN THE MORNING:**

Combine the pumpkin, garlic, ginger, lemongrass, water, bouillon, agave, turmeric, cumin, coriander, salt, and chili powder in the slow cooker. Cook on low for 6 to 8 hours.

About 20 minutes before serving, stir the coconut milk and lime zest into the soup. Taste and adjust the seasonings.

You can leave it chunky or purée with an immersion blender or in batches in a countertop blender, being careful of splatters of hot soup, depending on your preference.

YIELD: 8 servings
TOTAL PREP TIME: 10 minutes
TOTAL COOKING TIME: 6 to 8 hours

DID YOU KNOW?

Pumpkin is full of potassium, vitamin A, carotenoids, and beta-carotene.

HUNGARIAN MUSHROOM SOUP

▸ SOY-FREE ▸ GLUTEN-FREE

There is a special place in my heart for Mollie Katzen. I taught myself
how to cook from her *Moosewood Cookbook*. This is one of her recipes that
I have veganized and adapted to the slow cooker. It is a thick, super-creamy,
earthy treat on a cold winter's night. It's also one of my most requested soups.

....

FOR THE CASHEW SOUR CREAM:

¾ cup (100 g) raw cashews

½ cup (120 ml) water

Juice of ½ lemon

FOR THE SOUP:

2 tablespoons (30 ml) olive oil

1 medium-size onion, minced

2 packages (10 ounces, or 280 g each) mushrooms,
  chopped

2 cups (470 ml) water

½ tablespoon (3 g) vegan chicken-flavored bouillon or
  1 tablespoon (6 g) Chickeny Bouillon (page 19)

Juice of ½ lemon

Salt and pepper, to taste

1 to 2 tablespoons (4 g) minced dill (to taste),
  plus extra for garnish

2 tablespoons (14 g) paprika

☾ THE NIGHT BEFORE:

To make the sour cream: Combine the cashews, water, and
lemon juice in a blender or food processor and purée until
fairly smooth. Store in an airtight container in the fridge.

To make the soup: Heat the oil in a skillet over medium
heat. Add the onion and sauté until translucent, 3 to 5
minutes. Add the mushrooms and cook until they begin to
brown and give off their liquid, 8 to 10 minutes. Store in a
separate airtight container in the fridge.

☼ IN THE MORNING:

Combine the sautéed vegetables, water, bouillon, lemon
juice, salt and pepper, dill, and paprika in the slow cooker.
Cook on low for 6 to 8 hours.

Add the sour cream and stir to combine. Adjust the
seasonings to taste.

Garnish bowls of hot soup with extra dill.

YIELD: 4 servings
TOTAL PREP TIME: 15 minutes
TOTAL COOKING TIME: 6 to 8 hours

RECIPE IDEAS & VARIATIONS

Don't have any cashews on hand? Use the same
amount of silken tofu instead. It makes a great nondairy sour cream, too!

ASIAN TOFU SOUP

▶ GLUTEN-FREE*

This is a perfect soup to serve as an appetizer for the
Sweet and Sour Smoked Tofu (page 118), or for a light dinner with a salad.

INGREDIENTS:

1-inch (2.5 cm) piece peeled ginger, cut into large slices, divided

2 cloves garlic, minced

6 to 8 shiitake mushrooms, stems removed and caps sliced

1 block (15 ounces, or 420 g) tofu, drained and cut into cubes

2 tablespoons (12 g) vegan chicken-flavored bouillon or 4 tablespoons (24 g) Chickeny Bouillon (page 19)

1 to 2 teaspoons soy sauce (*use a gluten-free brand)

7 cups (1,645 ml) water

Sliced scallions or garlic chives, for serving

☾ THE NIGHT BEFORE:

Store the cut-up ginger, garlic, mushrooms, and tofu in an airtight container in the fridge.

☀ IN THE MORNING:

Combine half of the ginger, the garlic, mushrooms, tofu, bouillon, soy sauce, and water in the slow cooker. Cook on low for 6 to 8 hours.

About 30 minutes before serving, add the remaining half of the ginger and cook for 30 more minutes. Taste and adjust the seasonings. Add a little more fresh grated ginger if you need more punch. Top bowls of soup with the scallion.

YIELD: 4 servings
TOTAL PREP TIME: 10 minutes
TOTAL COOKING TIME: 6 to 8 hours

A WORTHY NOTE

Ginger is great for your stomach, so this is a good substitute for chicken soup when you are feeling under the weather.

TORTILLA SOUP

▶ SOY-FREE ▶ GLUTEN-FREE*

I just love tortilla soup and it's hard to find a good vegan version when you're out. Making a batch of this is a perfect excuse to stay in and save some money. You can make it as spicy as you want. After all, it's your kitchen.

INGREDIENTS:

1 tablespoon (15 ml) olive oil

1 medium-size onion, minced

2 cloves garlic, minced

1 can (28 ounces, or 784 g) diced or crushed tomatoes or 3 cups (680 g) Preserve-the-Harvest Diced Tomatoes (page 25)

3 tablespoons (48 g) tomato paste

4 cups (940 ml) water

Juice of ½ lime

1 tablespoon (1 g) chopped fresh cilantro, plus extra for garnish

1 teaspoon cumin

½ teaspoon chili powder

¼ cup (120 ml) tequila (optional)

1 teaspoon agave nectar or maple syrup

1 to 2 cups (225 to 450 g) cubed chicken-flavored seitan, store-bought or homemade (page 21, optional, for a heartier soup)

Salt and pepper, to taste

½ avocado, chopped and tossed with some lime juice and chili powder

Tortilla chips (*use gluten-free), slightly crushed, for serving

☾ THE NIGHT BEFORE:

Heat the oil in a skillet over medium heat and sauté the onion until translucent, 3 to 5 minutes. Add the garlic and sauté for 1 minute longer. Store in an airtight container in the fridge.

☼ IN THE MORNING:

Combine the sautéed onion, tomatoes, tomato paste, water, lime juice, cilantro, cumin, chili powder, tequila, agave, salt, and pepper in the slow cooker. Cook on low for 6 to 8 hours.

Purée the soup with an immersion blender or in batches in a countertop blender, being careful of splatters of hot soup, or leave the soup chunky. Taste and adjust the seasoning. Add optional seitan. Turn slow cooker to high, and cook until soup is warmed thoroughly.

Top bowls of hot soup with the avocado, crushed tortilla chips, and fresh cilantro.

YIELD: 4 servings
TOTAL PREP TIME: 15 minutes
TOTAL COOKING TIME: 6 to 8 hours

SERVING SUGGESTION

Serve this soup with a salad topped with black beans, green chiles, and salsa to make a complete meal.

HOT AND SOUR SOUP

▶ GLUTEN-FREE

It's hard to find vegan soups at Chinese takeouts in most areas.
This is the perfect cold and flu season soup. It clears those sinuses right up!
You can adjust the amount of spice until it's just right for you.

....

INGREDIENTS:

1 package (10 ounces, or 280 g) sliced mushrooms

8 fresh shiitake mushrooms, stems removed and
    caps sliced

1 can (8 ounces, or 225 g) bamboo shoots, drained
    and julienned

4 cloves garlic, minced

1 package (15 ounces, or 420 g) firm or silken tofu, cubed

2 tablespoons (16 g) grated fresh ginger, divided

4 cups (940 ml) water

2 tablespoons (12 g) vegan chicken-flavored bouillon
    or 4 tablespoons (24 g) Chickeny Bouillon (page 19)

2 tablespoons (30 ml) soy sauce

1 teaspoon sesame oil, plus extra for drizzling

1 teaspoon chili paste

2 tablespoons (30 ml) rice wine vinegar or apple
    cider vinegar

1½ cups (225 g) fresh or frozen peas

☾ THE NIGHT BEFORE:

Store the cut-up mushrooms, bamboo shoots, garlic, and
tofu in an airtight container in the fridge. Store the prepared ginger in another airtight container in the fridge.

☼ IN THE MORNING:

Combine the mushrooms, bamboo shoots, garlic, tofu,
1 tablespoon (8 g) of the ginger, water, bouillon, soy sauce,
sesame oil, chili paste, and vinegar in the slow cooker.
Cook on low for 8 hours.

A few minutes before serving, add the peas and the
remaining 1 tablespoon (8 g) ginger and stir to combine.
Taste the broth and add more vinegar or chili if needed.
Drizzle a few drops of sesame oil on top of each serving.
If you like it milder and your friends like it hot, serve the
chili paste on the side.

YIELD: 4 servings
TOTAL PREP TIME: 15 minutes
TOTAL COOKING TIME: 6 to 8 hours

SPLIT PEA AND APPLE SOUP

▸ SOY-FREE ▸ GLUTEN-FREE

I like the sweet and slightly tart taste of apples combined with the rich feel of split peas. It makes me feel like my split pea soup has really grown up. So indulge in this soup for your health or for a little cold-weather comfort food. It freezes well, and leftovers are perfect for lunches.

INGREDIENTS:

2 stalks celery, chopped

2 medium-size carrots, chopped

1 medium-size apple, peeled if not organic, cored, chopped, and tossed with lemon juice

1 clove garlic, minced

6 cups (1410 ml) water

2 tablespoons (12 g) vegan chicken-flavored bouillon or 4 tablespoons (24 g) Chickeny Bouillon (page 19)

2 cups (450 g) split peas

1 bay leaf

1 teaspoon dried thyme or 1 sprig of fresh

1 teaspoon coriander

$\frac{1}{2}$ teaspoon nutmeg (grate it fresh, if possible)

Salt, to taste

1 tablespoon (15 ml) balsamic vinegar, plus extra for drizzling

☾ THE NIGHT BEFORE:

Store the cut-up celery, carrots, apple, and garlic in an airtight container in the fridge.

☀ IN THE MORNING:

Combine the celery, carrots, apple, garlic, water, bouillon, split peas, bay leaf, thyme, coriander, nutmeg, and salt in the slow cooker. Cook on low for 6 to 8 hours.

Remove and discard the bay leaf and sprig of thyme. Add the balsamic vinegar and stir to combine. Purée the soup with an immersion blender or in batches in a countertop blender, being careful of splatters of hot soup, until smooth. Taste and adjust the seasonings, if needed. Drizzle a few drops of extra balsamic on each serving.

YIELD: 4 servings
TOTAL PREP TIME: 15 minutes
TOTAL COOKING TIME: 6 to 8 hours

DID YOU KNOW?

Split peas are full of soluble fiber, protein, and potassium.

DELICATA SQUASH AND PEAR SOUP

▶ SOY-FREE   ▶ GLUTEN-FREE

All winter squashes pair well with something a little sweet. I like mixing them
with fresh pears and apples in the winter to liven up a soup or casserole.
It's unexpected, and a nice change of pace during the colder months.

....

INGREDIENTS:

1 medium-size delicata or other winter squash

2 medium-size pears or apples

1 small onion, chopped

1 clove garlic, chopped

4 cups (940 ml) water

2 tablespoons (12 g) vegan chicken-flavored bouillon
    or 4 tablespoons (24 g) Chickeny Bouillon (page 19)

1 tablespoon (15 ml) port or red wine

1 sprig fresh thyme

1 sprig fresh rosemary

Salt and pepper, to taste

Finely chopped pistachios, for serving

Minced fresh thyme, for serving

☾ THE NIGHT BEFORE:

Cut the delicata squash in half, scrape the seeds out, and
then use a vegetable peeler to remove the skin. Chop the
flesh into cubes. Peel the pears, core, and chop. Toss with
lemon juice to prevent browning. Store the cut-up squash
and pears in an airtight container in the fridge.

☀ IN THE MORNING:

Combine all the ingredients in the slow cooker. Cook on
low for 6 to 8 hours.

Remove the thyme and rosemary sprigs. Purée the soup
with an immersion blender or in batches in a countertop blender, being careful of splatters of hot soup, until
smooth. Adjust the seasonings to taste, and add more
water or broth if needed. Top with pistachios and minced
fresh thyme.

YIELD: 6 servings
TOTAL PREP TIME: 15 minutes
TOTAL COOKING TIME: 6 to 8 hours

RECIPE IDEAS & VARIATIONS

My favorite combo is pear and delicata squash, but
use any winter squash you happen to have on hand to
create your own one-of-a-kind soup.

TURBODOG ROOT VEGGIE SOUP

► SOY-FREE ► GLUTEN-FREE*

Turbodog is a dark beer brewed by Abita Brewery just outside of New Orleans, Louisiana. All of the beers they brew are vegan and very tasty. The beer adds an almost caramel flavor to the broth. Feel free to mix and match the root veggies that are in season in your area. If turnips aren't your favorite, use a small one, and add extra of one of the other veggies. Or you can simply leave it out—it's your, soup after all!

Note: You want close to an equal amount of each veggie. The sizes will vary depending on the time of year, so just make sure you are selecting by the sizes that are available when shopping.

INGREDIENTS:

1 medium-size rutabaga

1 medium-size turnip

1 large golden beet

1 small celery root

1 medium-size parsnip

1 large carrot

2 cloves garlic, minced

2 cups (470 ml) water

1 bottle (12 ounces, or 355 ml) Abita Turbodog beer or your favorite vegan dark beer (*buy a gluten-free beer to make this gluten-free)

1 tablespoon (6 g) vegan chicken-flavored bouillon or 2 tablespoons (12 g) Chickeny Bouillon (page 19)

2 sprigs fresh thyme

1 sprig fresh rosemary

1 bay leaf

Salt and pepper, to taste

☾ THE NIGHT BEFORE:

Peel, trim the ends, and dice the rutabaga, turnip, beet, celery root, parsnip, and carrot. Store the cut-up vegetables in an airtight container in the fridge.

☀ IN THE MORNING:

Combine all the ingredients in the slow cooker. Cook on low for 6 to 8 hours. Remove and discard the thyme and rosemary sprigs and bay leaf. Taste and adjust the seasonings before serving.

YIELD: 4 to 6 servings
TOTAL PREP TIME: 15 minutes
TOTAL COOKING TIME: 6 to 8 hours

RECIPE IDEAS & VARIATIONS

Use red beets to tint the broth red. The taste will be the same, but the presentation is more dramatic. Plus, it's perfect for a Halloween dinner. Get some vegan pumpernickel bread, cut out with a cat-shaped cookie cutter, and toast. It's even more dramatic with a giant black cat crouton floating on top!

SPLIT PEA AND LENTIL SOUP

▸ SOY-FREE ▸ GLUTEN-FREE

When I first became a vegetarian, I had a soup that married split peas
and lentils with spinach. It was my favorite, but the recipe became lost over
the years. This is my redo of the wonderful memory of that warm, nutritious soup.

INGREDIENTS:

2 tablespoons (30 ml) olive oil

1 small onion, minced

1 cup (200 g) lentils

1 cup (200 g) split peas

6 cups (1410 ml) water

2 tablespoons (12 g) vegan chicken-flavored bouillon
or 4 tablespoons (24 g) Chickeny Bouillon (page 19)

2 bay leaves

1 teaspoon dried tarragon

½ teaspoon dried marjoram

¼ teaspoon ground rosemary or 1 teaspoon dried leaves

Salt and pepper, to taste

6 ounces (170 g) fresh baby spinach, washed

☾ THE NIGHT BEFORE:

Heat the oil in a skillet over medium heat and sauté the
onion until translucent, 3 to 5 minutes. Add the garlic and
sauté for 1 minute longer. Store in an airtight container in
the fridge.

☼ IN THE MORNING:

Combine the sautéed onion, lentils, peas, water, bouillon,
bay leaves, tarragon, marjoram, rosemary, and salt and
pepper in the slow cooker. Cook on low for 6 to 8 hours.

About 30 minutes before serving, add the spinach. Taste
and adjust the seasonings. Remove and discard the bay
leaves before serving.

YIELD: 8 servings
TOTAL PREP TIME: 15 minutes
TOTAL COOKING TIME: 6 to 8 hours

DID YOU KNOW?

Split peas and lentils are full of fiber, protein, iron,
magnesium, and zinc.

SMOKED TOFU AND STARS SOUP

▶ GLUTEN-FREE

This is my favorite soup when I'm sick. It's warm and filling,
and evokes memories of childhood soups with fun-shaped pasta.

INGREDIENTS:

2 tablespoons (30 ml) olive oil

1 medium-size onion, minced

4 cloves garlic, minced

2 carrots

2 stalks celery

1 package (8 ounces, or 225 g) smoked tofu or ¾ recipe
    Tea-Scented Tofu (page 24)

2 tablespoons (12 g) vegan chicken-flavored bouillon
    or 4 tablespoons (24 g) Chickeny Bouillon (page 19)

8 cups (1,880 ml) water

3 sprigs fresh thyme or 1 teaspoon dried

Salt and pepper, to taste

½ teaspoon Cajun seasoning (optional)

1 cup (100 g) small pasta stars or other tiny pasta

☪ THE NIGHT BEFORE:

Heat the oil in a skillet over medium heat and sauté
the onion until translucent, 3 to 5 minutes. Add the garlic
and sauté for 1 minute longer. Dice the carrots, celery, and
tofu. Store everything together in an airtight container in
the fridge.

☀ IN THE MORNING:

Combine the sautéed vegetables, carrots, celery, tofu,
bouillon, water, thyme, salt and pepper, and Cajun seasoning in the slow cooker. Cook on low for 6 to 8 hours. Taste
and adjust the seasonings.

You have two choices for adding the pasta. If you plan on
eating all of it that night, then add the pasta 20 minutes
before serving. Cook until the pasta is al dente. If you will
be eating it throughout the week or freezing it, cook the
pasta separately on the stove top and add it just before
serving. The pasta will get mushy if it stays in the soup
too long.

YIELD: 6 servings
TOTAL PREP TIME: 15 minutes
TOTAL COOKING TIME: 6 to 8 hours

WHAT'S IN THE FREEZER? VEGGIE SOUP

▶ SOY-FREE   ▶ GLUTEN-FREE

This is the easiest recipe you will ever make. Some mornings I only have 5 minutes to start some dinner in the slow cooker before I rush off to work. You can make this no matter what veggies you have on hand. I always keep a few bags of organic frozen veggies in the freezer for this soup, which you can serve chunky or puréed. Add parsnips, potato, or cauliflower if you want to make it look like a cream soup with none of the fat or calories!

INGREDIENTS:

6 cups mixed veggies (weight will vary depending on the veggies)

2 cloves garlic, minced

5 cups (1,175 ml) water

2 tablespoons (12 g) vegan chicken-flavored bouillon or 4 tablespoons (24 g) Chickeny Bouillon (page 19)

Your favorite combination of herbs and spices

Salt and pepper, to taste

2 to 4 cups (300 to 600 g) precooked grain or pasta

☼ IN THE MORNING:

Put any slow-cooking veggies, garlic, water, bouillon, herbs, spices, and salt and pepper in the slow cooker. Cook on low for 6 to 8 hours.

About 30 minutes before serving, add green peas, fresh herbs, or any other quick-cooking veggies, such as greens. This is also the time to add any precooked grain or pasta you may want to throw in to make it a little heartier. Taste and adjust the seasonings before serving.

YIELD: 6 servings
TOTAL PREP TIME: 5 minutes
TOTAL COOKING TIME: 6 to 8 hours

RECIPE IDEAS & VARIATIONS

- Try a few of these combos: sweet potato and ginger with thyme, curried cauliflower carrot, chunky Mexican chowder with fresh cilantro, and mixed vegetable soup with diced tomatoes and basil.

- Make it Asian style with a little soy sauce and fresh grated ginger. You can even top off your creation with a little sesame oil before serving.

- Not enough veggies in the freezer? Add canned or frozen beans instead.

CREAMY POTATO SOUP

▸ SOY-FREE ▸ GLUTEN-FREE

This is another one of my favorite comfort foods. It's great when you don't feel good, or if it's just chilly outside. It also makes an excellent base for other creamy soups, so add in some broccoli, spinach, or even carrots for an un-cream soup.

INGREDIENTS:

4 medium-size russet potatoes, peeled and cut into medium-size cubes

1 clove garlic, minced

2 cups (470 ml) water

2 tablespoons (12 g) vegan chicken-flavored bouillon or 4 tablespoons (24 g) Chickeny Bouillon (page 19)

1 sprig fresh rosemary

Salt and pepper, to taste

1 cup (235 ml) unsweetened nondairy milk

☾ THE NIGHT BEFORE:

Store the cut-up potatoes and garlic in an airtight container in the fridge.

☀ IN THE MORNING:

Combine the potatoes, garlic, water, bouillon, rosemary, and salt and pepper in the slow cooker. Cook on low for 6 to 8 hours.

Add the nondairy milk, remove and discard the rosemary, and purée the soup with an immersion blender or in batches in a countertop blender, being careful of splatters of hot soup, until smooth.

Taste and adjust the seasonings.

YIELD: 4 servings
TOTAL PREP TIME: 5 minutes
TOTAL COOKING TIME: 6 to 8 hours

SERVING SUGGESTION

Serve topped with vegan bacon bits, thinly sliced scallions, and some shredded vegan cheddar cheese.

CITRUS BLACK BEAN SOUP

▸ SOY-FREE ▸ GLUTEN-FREE

You get sweet and spicy flavors in this easy-to-make soup.

....

INGREDIENTS:

2 cloves garlic

4 cans (14½ ounces, or 406 g each) black beans, drained and rinsed, or 6 cups (1050 g) homemade (page 17)

1 can (14½ ounces, or 406 g) diced tomatoes or 1½ cups (340 g) Preserve-the-Harvest Diced Tomatoes (page 25)

1 tablespoon (7 g) jerk seasoning

1 teaspoon cumin

1 teaspoon chipotle chile powder

1 tablespoon (15 ml) liquid smoke

1 teaspoon to 1 tablespoon hot sauce (to taste)

Juice of 1 lime

Juice of 1 orange

1 tablespoon (1 g) chopped fresh cilantro

☪ **THE NIGHT BEFORE:**

Mince the garlic and store in an airtight container in the fridge.

☀ **IN THE MORNING:**

Combine the garlic, beans, tomatoes, jerk seasoning, cumin, chipotle, liquid smoke, hot sauce, lime juice, and orange juice in the slow cooker. Cook on low for about 8 hours.

If desired, purée the soup with an immersion blender or in batches in a countertop blender, being careful of splatters of hot soup, until smooth, or leave the soup chunky. Taste and adjust the seasonings. Serve topped with the chopped cilantro.

YIELD: 6 to 8 servings
TOTAL PREP TIME: 10 minutes
TOTAL COOKING TIME: 6 to 8 hours

SERVING SUGGESTION

I like to serve it as a first course at dinner parties. After all, my slow cooker keeps it warm right up to the time I serve it, so I can have it ready to go before my guests arrive.

CHAPTER 4

STEAMY STEWS AND CURRIES THAT SAVE THE DAY

Stews and curries are incredibly versatile and make great one-pot meals. Their flavors meld together with long cooking times and are perfect for cooking all day while you are at work. The curries are also wonderful served over rice, and all make for leftovers to look forward to!

If your slow cooker runs hot, you will need to add 1 to 2 cups (235 to 470 ml) of extra liquid. You'll also need to taste and adjust the seasonings before serving, because depending on the age of your herbs and how long you cook your stew, their flavors may fade and need a boost.

These recipes are perfect for doing most of the prep work at night before you go to bed. Then when you wake up in the morning it takes very little time to get your dish in the slow cooker. Once you get used to coming home to a ready-made hot dinner, it's hard to remember why you weren't doing this before. Less going out means eating healthier and less expensive food.

1. Soy Chorizo Black Bean Stew
2. White Bean and Kale Stew
3. Asian-Style Winter Stew
4. Veggie Gumbo with Cheater Roux
5. Mojito Pinto Beans
6. Cheater Chili
7. Tofu Bouillabaisse
8. Chinese-Style Eggplant in Garlic Sauce
9. Hard Cider and Cabbage Stew
10. Thai Red Curry Tofu and Veggies
11. Caribbean Mango Black Beans
12. Not-My-Grandmother's Beefy Stew
13. Sweet Potato and Chard Dal
14. Chana Saag (Indian Greens with Chickpeas)
15. Baigan Bharta (Eggplant Curry)
16. Easy Veggie Chickpea Biryani
17. Butter Chick'n

SOY CHORIZO BLACK BEAN STEW

The complex flavor of the chorizo is grounded with black beans and sautéed veggies. Serve with tortillas or chips to dip in the stew.

INGREDIENTS:

1 tablespoon (15 ml) olive oil

1 small onion, minced

1 clove garlic, minced

½ bell pepper, minced

½ package (6 ounces, or 170 g) soy chorizo

2 cans (15 ounces, or 420 g each) black beans, drained and rinsed, or 3 cups (520 g) homemade (page 17)

2 cups (470 ml) water

1½ tablespoons (9 g) vegan chicken-flavored bouillon or 3 tablespoons (18 g) Chickeny Bouillon (page 19)

¼ teaspoon cumin

¼ teaspoon chipotle or pasilla chile powder

Salt and pepper, to taste

☾ THE NIGHT BEFORE:

Heat the oil in a skillet over medium heat and sauté the onion until translucent, 3 to 5 minutes. Add the garlic and bell pepper and sauté for 3 minutes longer. Store the sautéed vegetables in an airtight container in the fridge.

☼ IN THE MORNING:

Combine all the ingredients in the slow cooker. Cook on low for 6 to 8 hours. Taste and adjust the seasonings before serving. Top with cilantro if desired.

YIELD: 4 servings
TOTAL PREP TIME: 10 minutes
TOTAL COOKING TIME: 6 to 8 hours

SERVING SUGGESTION

Use leftovers in tacos or burritos.

WHITE BEAN AND KALE STEW

▸ SOY-FREE ▸ GLUTEN-FREE

I like my beans New Orleans style—thick and creamy. I've found the easiest vegan
way to do this is to let some of the beans break down and form their own gravy.

INGREDIENTS:

1 teaspoon olive oil

1 onion, chopped

2 cloves garlic, minced

Salt and pepper, to taste

1 tablespoon (15 ml) balsamic vinegar

4 cups (270 g) washed and chopped kale

1 tablespoon (4 g) chopped fresh oregano or
    1 teaspoon dried

5 cups (1,175 ml) water

2 cans (14½ ounces, or 406 g each) white beans, drained
    and rinsed, or 3 cups (520 g) homemade (page 17)

☾ THE NIGHT BEFORE:

Heat the oil in a skillet over medium heat and sauté the
onion until translucent, 3 to 5 minutes. Add the garlic and
a little salt and pepper and sauté for 1 to 2 minutes longer.
Add the balsamic vinegar and stir to combine. Store the
sautéed onion and the cut-up kale in separate airtight
containers in the fridge.

☼ IN THE MORNING:

Combine the sautéed onion, oregano, water, and beans
in the slow cooker. Cook on low for 6 to 8 hours.

About 30 minutes before serving, add the kale. Cook for
30 minutes longer, then taste and adjust the seasonings
before serving.

YIELD: 6 servings
TOTAL PREP TIME: 15 minutes
TOTAL COOKING TIME: 6 to 8 hours

RECIPE IDEAS & VARIATIONS

If you are not a kale lover you can substitute any
green you happen to like (or is ready to pick in your
garden). Start by adding 2 cups (135 g) kale instead
of 4 cups (270 g) and work your way up. Greens are a
nutritional powerhouse and are worth getting used to!

ASIAN-STYLE WINTER STEW

This is a hearty stew that can be made with staples and veggies in your pantry.
It's perfect for a snowy day, when you can't (or just don't want to) go to the store.
It's a warming root stew flavored with miso, then topped with sesame oil.

INGREDIENTS:

2 tablespoons (30 ml) olive oil

1 medium-size onion, cut in half and sliced

2 cloves garlic, minced

1 tablespoon (8 g) grated ginger

1 small turnip, chopped

3-inch (7.5 cm) piece daikon, chopped

8 baby or fingerling potatoes, cut in half if large

8 ounces (225 g) baby carrots, cut in half if large

4 ounces (113 g) mushrooms (I use a packaged
    blend of baby bella, shiitake, and oyster), cut
    into large chunks

2 tablespoons (12 g) vegan chicken-flavored bouillon
    or 4 tablespoons (24 g) Chickeny Bouillon (page 19)

2 tablespoons (32 g) miso

1 cup (235 ml) water

Salt and pepper, to taste

Sesame oil, for serving

☾ THE NIGHT BEFORE:

Heat the oil in a skillet over medium heat and sauté the onion until translucent, 3 to 5 minutes. Add the garlic and sauté for 3 minutes longer. Combine the sautéed onion, grated ginger, and cut-up vegetables in a large airtight container and store in the refrigerator.

☀ IN THE MORNING:

Combine all the ingredients in the slow cooker. Cook on low for 6 to 8 hours. Remove and discard the bay leaves. Taste and adjust the seasonings. Serve drizzled with sesame oil.

YIELD: 4 servings
TOTAL PREP TIME: 15 minutes
TOTAL COOKING TIME: 6 to 8 hours

RECIPE IDEAS & VARIATIONS

Add some chile paste if you like some heat. It's also a great way to warm up after a snowball fight!

VEGGIE GUMBO WITH CHEATER ROUX

In New Orleans, everyone has his or her own variation on gumbo. It started as a way to use leftovers and make a full meal out of a not-so-full pantry. This recipe is unique because it replaces a slow-cooked traditional roux with a simple thickener that takes less time than the slow browning method, but still retains a smoky flavor.

FOR THE GUMBO:

2 tablespoons (30 ml) olive oil

1 small onion, minced

2 cloves garlic, minced

2 stalks celery, minced

2 medium-size bell peppers, chopped

1½ cups (165 g) chopped vegan Italian sausage, tempeh, or tofu

12 ounces (340 g) okra

1 can (14½ ounces, or 406 g) diced tomatoes or 1½ cups (340 g) Preserve-the-Harvest Diced Tomatoes (page 25)

4 cups (940 ml) water

3 tablespoons (18 g) vegan chicken-flavored bouillon or 6 tablespoons (36 g) Chickeny Bouillon (page 19)

1 teaspoon Cajun seasoning

FOR THE CHEATER ROUX:

6 roasted or smoked almonds

1 cup (225 g) white beans, drained and rinsed

¼ teaspoon liquid smoke

1 to 3 teaspoons water

Cooked rice, for serving

☾ THE NIGHT BEFORE:

To make the gumbo: Heat the oil in a skillet over medium heat and sauté the onion until translucent, 3 to 5 minutes. Add the garlic and celery and sauté for 3 minutes longer. Store the sautéed vegetables and the cut-up bell peppers and sausage together in an airtight container in the fridge.

To make the roux: Place the almonds in a food processor and process until coarse. Add the white beans and liquid smoke and process again. Add the water, 1 teaspoon at a time, until the mixture comes together and blends thoroughly. Store the roux in a separate airtight container in the fridge.

☀ IN THE MORNING:

Slice the okra. Combine the okra, sautéed vegetables, bell peppers, sausage, tomatoes, water, bouillon, and Cajun seasoning in the slow cooker. Cook on low for 6 to 8 hours.

About 20 minutes before serving, stir the roux into the gumbo. Heat through, then taste and adjust the seasonings.

Ladle the gumbo into bowls, then add a scoop of rice to each one, like an island in the middle of the bowl, and serve.

YIELD: 6 servings
TOTAL PREP TIME: 15 minutes
TOTAL COOKING TIME: 6 to 8 hours

MOJITO PINTO BEANS

▸ SOY-FREE ▸ GLUTEN-FREE

Lime, rum, and mint come together to create a bold flavor in these beans. As the rum cooks down with the beans, it creates a rich sauce. The lime juice and mint really brighten up the dish. If you haven't used mint in savory dishes before, add a small amount at first. Serve over rice with a side of steamed veggies for a complete meal.

INGREDIENTS:

1 small onion

2 cans (15 ounces, or 420 g each) pinto beans, drained and rinsed, or 3 cups (520 g) homemade (page 17)

½ cup (120 ml) water

½ cup (120 ml) rum (dark is best)

½ teaspoon cumin

½ tablespoon (3 g) vegan chicken-flavored bouillon or 1 tablespoon (6 g) Chickeny Bouillon (page 19)

1 tablespoon (16 g) tomato paste

Juice of 1 lime

Salt and pepper, to taste

Chopped fresh mint, for serving

☾ THE NIGHT BEFORE:

Dice the onion and store in an airtight container in the fridge.

☀ IN THE MORNING:

Combine all the ingredients in the slow cooker. Cook on low for 6 to 8 hours.

Taste and adjust the seasonings, then top with the chopped mint.

YIELD: 4 small servings
TOTAL PREP TIME: 10 minutes
TOTAL COOKING TIME: 6 to 8 hours

DID YOU KNOW?

The mint family includes basil, lemon balm, oregano, sweet marjoram, and sage.

CHEATER CHILI

▸ SOY-FREE ▸ GLUTEN-FREE

If you need to throw together a quick dinner before you dash out the door, this is the recipe for you. It's simple, and you can raid your pantry for cans or look in the freezer for ingredients you've put up yourself.

INGREDIENTS:

1 can (14½ ounces, or 406 g) black beans, drained and rinsed, or 1½ cups (340 g) homemade (page 17)

1 can (14½ ounces, or 406 g) pinto beans, drained and rinsed, or 1½ cups (340 g) homemade (page 17)

1 can (14½ ounces, or 406 g) kidney beans, drained and rinsed, or 1½ cups (340 g) homemade (page 17)

1 can (14½ ounces, or 406 g) corn, drained and rinsed, or 1½ cups (195 g) frozen

1 can (28 ounces, or 784 g) diced tomatoes or 3 cups (680 g) Preserve-the-Harvest Diced Tomatoes (page 25)

3 cloves garlic, minced, or ½ teaspoon garlic powder

1 tablespoon (7.5 g) chili powder

A few dashes liquid smoke

A few dashes Tabasco sauce (to taste)

Salt and pepper, to taste

DIRECTIONS:

Combine all the ingredients in the slow cooker. Cook on low for 6 to 8 hours. Taste and adjust the seasonings.

YIELD: 6 servings
TOTAL PREP TIME: 5 minutes
TOTAL COOKING TIME: 6 to 8 hours

RECIPE IDEAS & VARIATIONS

This is a basic chili recipe, but feel free to add some frozen veggies to the mix as well. I keep some frozen onion and pepper strips just for such an occasion.

TOFU BOUILLABAISSE

This is a fragrant, tomato-based stew cooked with saffron and fresh fennel. The potatoes and tofu make it a hearty meal that will even please your nonvegan friends.

INGREDIENTS:

2 tablespoons (30 ml) olive oil

1 medium-size onion, cut in half and sliced

3 cloves garlic, minced

½ medium-size fennel bulb, chopped

3 stalks celery, chopped

2 carrots, cut into half-moons

3 medium-size potatoes, cut into chunks

1 package (15 ounces, or 420 g) extra-firm tofu, cubed

1 can (28 ounces, or 784 g) diced tomatoes or 3 cups (540 g) chopped fresh

1½ cups (353 ml) water

2 bay leaves

½ teaspoon saffron

Salt and pepper, to taste

Zest and juice of ½ lime

☾ THE NIGHT BEFORE:

Heat the oil in a skillet over medium heat and sauté the onion until translucent, 3 to 5 minutes. Add the garlic and sauté for 3 minutes longer. Store the sautéed onion and the cut-up fennel, celery, carrots, potatoes, and tofu in an airtight container in the fridge.

☀ IN THE MORNING:

Combine all the ingredients in the slow cooker. Cook on low for 6 to 8 hours. Taste and adjust the seasonings. Remove the bay leaves before serving.

YIELD: 6 servings
TOTAL PREP TIME: 15 minutes
TOTAL COOKING TIME: 6 to 8 hours

RECIPE IDEAS & VARIATIONS

You can add seaweed, such as Kombu, for some sea flavor, if you like. Just add it in the morning with the other ingredients.

CHINESE-STYLE EGGPLANT IN GARLIC SAUCE

▶ GLUTEN-FREE*

This is a variation on my favorite Chinese takeout dish. You can make it with any kind of eggplant, but it looks amazing using the tiny Fairy Tale variety. Just remove the tops and cook them whole. Be sure to use large chunks or whole small eggplants and note the shorter cooking time.

INGREDIENTS:

1½ pounds (681 g) eggplant (Italian, Japanese, Indian, Fairy Tale, or other variety)

Sesame oil, for serving

FOR THE SAUCE:

4 cloves garlic, minced

2 tablespoons (16 g) fresh grated ginger

½ to 1 cup (120 to 235 ml) water (use the larger amount if your slow cooker runs hot)

1½ tablespoons (9 g) vegan chicken-flavored bouillon or 3 tablespoons (18 g) Chickeny Bouillon (page 19)

2 tablespoons (30 ml) soy sauce (*use gluten-free)

2 tablespoons (30 ml) hoisin sauce (*use gluten-free)

2 to 3 tablespoons (30 to 45 ml) agave nectar or maple syrup (to taste)

½ to 1 teaspoon sriracha chili sauce (optional)

☾ THE NIGHT BEFORE:

Depending on the variety and size of your eggplants, you can leave them whole (Indian or Fairy Tale variety) or cut into large chunks.

To make the sauce: Combine all the sauce ingredients in a small bowl and mix thoroughly. Combine the sauce and the eggplant in a large airtight container and store in the refrigerator.

☀ IN THE MORNING:

Oil the crock of your slow cooker and add the eggplant and sauce. Cook on low for 5 to 6 hours, longer if you have an older slow cooker. Taste and add more soy sauce or sweetener if needed. Serve topped with a drizzle of sesame oil.

YIELD: 4 servings
TOTAL PREP TIME: 10 minutes
TOTAL COOKING TIME: 5 to 6 hours

RECIPE IDEAS & VARIATIONS

This is a great way to try out all kinds of eggplant. Try orange, lavender, or white ones for a change of pace.

HARD CIDER AND CABBAGE STEW

This is a sausage and veggie stew that tastes like fall itself. The hard cider mellows out while cooking and makes for a perfect, savory broth.

INGREDIENTS:

2 tablespoons (30 ml) olive oil

1 small onion, chopped

3 cloves garlic, minced

2 medium-size carrots, sliced into coins

1 small head cabbage (about 14½ ounces, or 406 g), cored and chopped

1 small apple, peeled, cored, and diced

1 package (12 ounces, or 340 g) vegan sausage links (I used Wheat Roast brand smoked apple sage), sliced

2 cups (470 ml) hard cider

2 tablespoons (12 g) vegan chicken-flavored bouillon or 4 tablespoons (24 g) Chickeny Bouillon (page 19)

2 bay leaves

1 sprig rosemary

2 sprigs thyme

Salt and pepper, to taste

☾ THE NIGHT BEFORE:

Heat the oil in a skillet over medium heat and sauté the onion until translucent, 3 to 5 minutes. Add the garlic and sauté for 3 minutes longer. Combine the sautéed onion and cut-up vegetables, apple, and sausage in a large air-tight container and store in the refrigerator.

☀ IN THE MORNING:

Combine all the ingredients in the slow cooker. Cook on low for 6 to 8 hours. Remove and discard the bay leaves, rosemary sprig, and thyme sprigs. Taste and adjust the seasonings.

YIELD: 6 servings
TOTAL PREP TIME: 15 minutes
TOTAL COOKING TIME: 6 to 8 hours

RECIPE IDEAS & VARIATIONS

If you are avoiding gluten, use smoked tofu instead, and add ½ teaspoon rubbed sage to the recipe.

THAI RED CURRY TOFU AND VEGGIES

Thai curry paste can be found in most groceries, and most are vegan.
Use less curry paste if you like milder foods and more if you like it fiery hot.

INGREDIENTS:

1 large onion, minced

1 bell pepper, julienned

1 can (8 ounces, or 225 g) bamboo shoots, drained and julienned

½ head cauliflower, cut into florets

1½ packages (15 ounces, or 420 g each) extra-firm tofu, cubed

½ head broccoli, cut into florets

1 to 2 tablespoons (16 to 32 g) red curry paste

2 cups (470 ml) water

Juice of 1 lime

1 can (14 ounces, or 392 g) light coconut milk

Fresh Thai basil, for serving

1 lime, sliced, for serving

☾ **THE NIGHT BEFORE:**

Store the cut-up onion, bell pepper, bamboo shoots, and cauliflower, and tofu in an airtight container in the fridge. Store the cut-up broccoli in a separate airtight container in the fridge.

☀ **IN THE MORNING:**

Combine the onion, bell pepper, bamboo shoots, cauliflower, tofu, curry paste, water, and lime juice in the slow cooker. Cook on low for 6 to 8 hours.

About 20 minutes before serving, add the coconut milk and broccoli. Cook until the broccoli is tender. Taste and adjust the seasonings. Serve topped with chopped Thai basil and a slice of lime.

YIELD: 6 servings
TOTAL PREP TIME: 15 minutes
TOTAL COOKING TIME: 6 to 8 hours

RECIPE IDEAS & VARIATIONS

Swap out the veggies depending on the season. Zucchini, acorn squash, green beans, and kale, all make tasty additions.

CARIBBEAN MANGO BLACK BEANS

▶ SOY-FREE ▶ GLUTEN-FREE

Sometimes you need something easy to make that's good enough for company. These beans have a hint of sweetness from the mango with a layer of spiciness underneath. You can halve this recipe if you aren't serving a crowd, or you can freeze the leftovers for another night. Serve over rice, in a burrito, or by themselves as a side.

INGREDIENTS:

3 cloves garlic

2 mangoes

4 cans (15 ounces, or 420 g each) black beans, drained and rinsed, or 6 cups (1,040 g) homemade (page 17)

1 cup (235 ml) water

2 tablespoons (12 g) vegan chicken-flavored bouillon or 4 tablespoons (24 g) Chickeny Bouillon (page 19)

3 tablespoons (24 g) grated fresh ginger

1½ teaspoons paprika

2 teaspoons thyme

¼ teaspoon nutmeg

⅛ teaspoon ground cloves

⅛ teaspoon allspice

⅛ to ½ teaspoon ground hot pepper (to taste)

Salt and pepper, to taste

☾ THE NIGHT BEFORE:

Mince the garlic. Cut along both sides of the mango pit to remove 2 cheeks. Using your knife, cut lengthwise into the mango just to the skin. Do the same across widthwise, so that you have a checkerboard. Take the piece in hand and open the crisscross section so it bows out. Now take your knife and run it under the flesh. The fruit will easily fall off into chunks. Repeat with the remaining mango cheek. Store in an airtight container in the fridge.

☀ IN THE MORNING:

Oil the crock of your slow cooker and add all the ingredients. Cook on low for 6 to 8 hours. Taste and adjust the seasonings.

YIELD: 8 servings
TOTAL PREP TIME: 10 minutes
TOTAL COOKING TIME: 6 to 8 hours

NOT-MY-GRANDMOTHER'S BEEFY STEW

▶ SOY-FREE

This is the stew I imagine I would have grown up on if my grandmother had been a vegan. Beefy seitan is combined with potatoes, carrots, and sweet potatoes for a filling winter meal. The sweet potatoes cook down into a sauce flavored with rosemary and thyme. This recipe may be a little big for a 3½-quart (3.3 L) slow cooker, but you can easily halve the recipe.

INGREDIENTS:

2 cloves garlic, minced

3 carrots, cut into half-moons

1 small sweet potato, cut into chunks

8 baby potatoes, cut into quarters

4 cups (440 g) cubed beef-flavored seitan, store-bought or homemade (page 22)

1 cup (235 ml) water

2 tablespoons (12 g) vegan beef-flavored bouillon or 4 tablespoons (24 g) Beefy Bouillon (page 20)

2 sprigs fresh thyme

1 sprig rosemary

½ teaspoon Cajun seasoning (optional)

Salt and pepper, to taste

☾ THE NIGHT BEFORE:

Store the cut-up garlic, carrots, sweet potato, potatoes, and seitan in an airtight container in the fridge.

☀ IN THE MORNING:

Combine all the ingredients in the slow cooker. Cook on low for 6 to 8 hours. Remove and discard the thyme and rosemary sprigs. Taste and adjust the seasonings.

YIELD: 6 servings
TOTAL PREP TIME: 15 minutes
TOTAL COOKING TIME: 6 to 8 hours

RECIPE IDEAS & VARIATIONS

Use five dried mushrooms ground in a spice grinder or blender to replace the beef-flavored bouillon if you don't have any on hand. It adds a similar dark flavor to the stew and it contains no soy.

SWEET POTATO AND CHARD DAL

▸ SOY-FREE ▸ GLUTEN-FREE

No Indian meal is complete without a bean dish. This dal, or lentil soup,
gets a nutritional boost from the sweet potato and chard. Serve over rice.

INGREDIENTS:

1 tablespoon (15 ml) olive oil

1 small onion, minced

1 teaspoon garam masala

¼ teaspoon turmeric

¼ teaspoon cumin

Pinch of chili powder

Salt, to taste

1 large sweet potato, diced

1 bunch Swiss chard, washed, chopped, and spun dry

1½ cups (338 g) yellow split peas

4 cups (940 ml) water

☾ THE NIGHT BEFORE:

Heat the oil in a skillet over medium heat and sauté the
onion with the garam masala, turmeric, cumin, chili powder, and salt until translucent, 3 to 5 minutes. Store in an
airtight container in the refrigerator. Combine the cut-up
vegetables in a separate airtight container and store in
the refrigerator.

☼ IN THE MORNING:

Combine the sautéed onion, sweet potato, split peas, and
water in the slow cooker. Cook on low for 6 to 8 hours.

About 20 minutes before serving, add the chard and
cook until tender, about 20 minutes. Taste and adjust the
seasonings.

YIELD: 6 servings
TOTAL PREP TIME: 20 minutes
TOTAL COOKING TIME: 6 to 8 hours

SERVING SUGGESTION

Indian meals are made up of a variety of dishes.
Try serving this soup with Baigan Bharta (page 82),
Chana Saag (page 80), or Butter Chick'n, (page 85).

CHANA SAAG (INDIAN GREENS WITH CHICKPEAS)

▶ SOY-FREE ▶ GLUTEN-FREE

You can use any combinations of greens here, such as spinach, Swiss chard, turnip greens, and collards, or anything that's plentiful where you live.

INGREDIENTS:

2 tablespoons (30 ml) olive oil

1 small onion, minced

2 cloves garlic, minced

1 tablespoon (8 g) grated fresh ginger

1 pound (454 g) assorted greens, washed, torn into bite-size pieces, and spun dry (you can also buy a prewashed mix in a bag)

Zest of 1/2 lime

1 teaspoon cumin powder

1/2 teaspoon turmeric

1/2 teaspoon ground coriander

1/2 teaspoon garam masala (or to taste)

1 1/2 cups (353 ml) water

2 tablespoons (12 g) vegan chicken-flavored bouillon or 4 tablespoons (24 g) Chickeny Bouillon (page 19)

1 can (15 ounces, or 420 g) chickpeas, drained and rinsed, or 1 1/2 cups (340 g) homemade (page 17)

1/2 to 1 cup (120 to 235 ml) plain nondairy creamer or nondairy milk

Salt, to taste

Rice, for serving

☾ THE NIGHT BEFORE:

Heat the oil in a skillet over medium heat and sauté the onion until translucent, 3 to 5 minutes. Add the garlic and sauté for 2 minutes longer. Store the sautéed onion, grated ginger, and prepared greens in an airtight container in the refrigerator. Store the lime zest separately in the fridge.

☼ IN THE MORNING:

Oil the crock of your slow cooker. Combine the sautéed onion, ginger, greens, spices, water, and bouillon in the slow cooker. Cook on low for 6 to 8 hours

About 30 minutes before serving, purée the soup with an immersion blender or in batches in a countertop blender, being careful of splatters of hot soup, until smooth. Add the chickpeas, nondairy creamer, lime zest, and salt to the slow cooker. Cook on high for 30 more minutes, until the beans are heated through. Taste and adjust the seasonings. Serve over rice.

YIELD: 6 servings
TOTAL PREP TIME: 15 minutes
TOTAL COOKING TIME: 6 to 8 hours

RECIPE IDEAS & VARIATIONS

- Add 1 or 2 chopped mild chiles during the last 30 minutes of cooking to give it more heat.

- Don't like chickpeas? Substitute 1/2 package (15 ounces, or 420 g) soft, firm, or extra-firm tofu, pressed and then cut into cubes. It will mimic a popular dish called saag paneer.

BAIGAN BHARTA (EGGPLANT CURRY)

▶ SOY-FREE ▶ GLUTEN-FREE

When eggplant cooks down it gets an almost creamy consistency. Add extra chipotle chile powder to make it spicier, or use a different type of chili to omit the smokiness.

INGREDIENTS:

2 tablespoons (30 ml) olive oil

1 small onion, minced

2 cloves garlic, minced

2 teaspoons grated ginger

4½ cups (about 1 pound, or 454 g) chopped eggplant

1 cup (235 ml) water

Salt, to taste

½ teaspoon garam masala

1 teaspoon cumin

½ teaspoon turmeric

Pinch of chipotle chile powder

☾ THE NIGHT BEFORE:

Heat the oil in a skillet over medium heat and sauté the onion until translucent, 3 to 5 minutes. Add the garlic and sauté for 2 minutes longer. Combine the sautéed onion, grated ginger, and cut-up eggplant in an airtight container and store in the fridge.

☀ IN THE MORNING:

Combine all the ingredients in the slow cooker. Cook on low for 6 to 8 hours. Taste and adjust the seasonings.

YIELD: 6 servings
TOTAL PREP TIME: 15 minutes
TOTAL COOKING TIME: 6 to 8 hours

SERVING SUGGESTION

Serve over brown basmati rice with Butter Chick'n (page 85).

EASY VEGGIE CHICKPEA BIRYANI

▶ SOY-FREE ▶ GLUTEN-FREE

This is made differently than a traditional biryani. Here we cook the veggies in a stew, then sandwich the stew between layers of cooked rice, instead of cooking the stew between the rice layers in the oven. It has all of the flavor, and if you have a rice cooker you won't heat up the kitchen at all.

....

INGREDIENTS:

2 tablespoons (30 ml) olive oil

1 small onion, minced

1 bell pepper, diced

1 teaspoon grated ginger

1 small sweet potato, diced

8 ounces (225 g) fresh or frozen cauliflower, broken into small florets

2 teaspoons garam masala

1 teaspoon cumin

1 teaspoon turmeric

½ teaspoon cinnamon

2 cups (470 ml) water

2 tablespoons (12 g) vegan chicken-flavored bouillon or 4 tablespoons (24 g) Chickeny Bouillon (page 19)

1 can (15 ounces, or 420 g) chickpeas, drained and rinsed, or 1½ cups (340 g) homemade (page 17)

Salt, to taste

4 to 6 cups (660 to 990 g) cooked rice (cook with a pinch of saffron if you have some on hand)

☾ THE NIGHT BEFORE:

Heat the oil in a skillet over medium heat and sauté the onion until translucent, 3 to 5 minutes. Add the bell pepper and cook for 2 minutes longer. Store the sautéed vegetables, the grated ginger, and the cut-up sweet potato and cauliflower together in a large airtight container in the refrigerator.

☀ IN THE MORNING:

Oil the crock of your slow cooker. Combine the sautéed vegetables, ginger, sweet potato, cauliflower, spices, water, bouillon, chickpeas, and salt in the slow cooker. Cook on low for 6 to 8 hours.

Taste and adjust the seasonings. Spread half of the cooked rice on a platter, cover with veggie chickpea stew, and top with the rest of the rice.

YIELD: 6 servings
TOTAL PREP TIME: 15 minutes
TOTAL COOKING TIME: 6 to 8 hours

BUTTER CHICK'N

▸ SOY-FREE* ▸ GLUTEN-FREE

This is a full-flavored curry sauce that can be served traditionally over a protein such as tofu, tempeh, or seitan. It also works great over steamed veggies, beans, or rice.

INGREDIENTS:

2 tablespoons (30 ml) olive oil

1 large onion, minced

4 cloves garlic, minced

2 tablespoons (16 g) grated ginger

1 can (28 ounces, or 784 g) diced tomatoes or 3 cups (540 g) fresh chopped

1½ to 2 tablespoons (11 to 14 g) garam masala (to taste)

1½ teaspoons cumin

⅛ teaspoon turmeric

Salt, to taste

¼ to ½ cup (60 to 120 ml) water (use the lower amount if you use the nondairy milk instead of the nondairy creamer)

1 package (15 ounces, or 420 g) tofu, drained and cubed (*substitute a similar amount of seitan or kidney beans to make this soy-free)

3 tablespoons (42 g) nondairy butter

¼ cup (60 ml) plain nondairy creamer or nondairy milk

Chopped fresh cilantro, for serving

Brown basmati rice, for serving

☾ THE NIGHT BEFORE:

Heat the oil in a skillet over medium heat and sauté the onion until translucent, 3 to 5 minutes. Add the garlic and sauté for 2 minutes longer. Store the sautéed onion and the grated ginger together in an airtight container in the refrigerator.

☀ IN THE MORNING:

Combine the sautéed onion, ginger, tomatoes, garam masala, cumin, turmeric, salt, water, and tofu in the slow cooker. Cook on low for 6 to 8 hours.

Just before serving, add the nondairy creamer and non-dairy butter and stir to combine and melt the butter. Taste and adjust the seasonings. Serve topped with a handful of chopped fresh cilantro over rice.

YIELD: 6 servings
TOTAL PREP TIME: 15 minutes
TOTAL COOKING TIME: 6 to 8 hours

CHAPTER 5

CASSEROLES (AND LOAVES) YOU WISH YOUR MOTHER HAD MADE

Casseroles are a staple at my house. I love a good one-dish meal that I can whip up in a few minutes. Some of these recipes work for an away-from-home day, and others cook in about 2 hours and fit better in a weekend lunch or dinner menu.

When the weather gets cooler and daylight saving time makes me miss my evening sunshine, I need all the comfort I can get. Although I was never much of a fan of meatloaf growing up, my twenty-seven years of living meatless has given me a love of veggie loaves. They're a good excuse to make mashed potatoes, and the leftovers are great in sandwiches. You can make a loaf right in the slow cooker crock, or you can use a loaf pan that fits into your slow cooker. It will take a little longer in the loaf pan because the end product will be thicker. I have lids for mine though, so it makes it easy to store the leftovers.

Stews that are topped with biscuits or include dumplings are perfect workday dinners because they start their lives as stews and you add the quick-cooking parts right before you are ready to eat.

1. Chick'n and Dumplings
2. From-the-Pantry Pot Pie
3. Chili Relleno Casserole
4. Chorizo and Sweet Potato Enchilada Casserole
5. Chick'n Mushroom Casserole
6. Italian Eggplant Casserole with Cashew-Tofu Ricotta
7. Better-than-the-Classic Shepherd's Pie
8. Atomic Tofu Pecan Loaf
9. Corn-tastic Tex-Mex Loaf
10. Holiday Tempeh and Sage Loaf

CHICK'N AND DUMPLINGS

It takes a little time and effort to make the dumplings, but it's well worth it.
Gluten and soy intolerant? Try using a can of chickpeas instead of the seitan.
Make it gluten-free by using a gluten-free baking mix instead of flour.

FOR THE STEW:

1½ cups (340 g) cubed chicken-flavored seitan, store-bought or homemade (page 21), or tofu marinated in 2 tablespoons (12 g) vegan chicken-flavored bouillon or 4 tablespoons (24 g) Chickeny Bouillon (page 19) and 1 cup (235 ml) water

6 medium-size carrots, chopped

2 large stalks celery or 2 sprigs lovage, chopped

4 cups (940 ml) vegan chicken broth or 4 cups (940 ml) water mixed with 2 tablespoons (12 g) vegan chicken-flavored bouillon or 4 tablespoons (24 g) Chickeny Bouillon (page 19)

1 bay leaf

3 sprigs fresh thyme

1 sprig rosemary

Salt and pepper, to taste

FOR THE DUMPLINGS:

2 cups (250 g) flour (white, whole wheat, or gluten-free baking mix)

1 teaspoon salt (optional)

1 teaspoon dried thyme

Pinch of baking powder

1 cup (235 ml) plain or unsweetened nondairy milk

☽ THE NIGHT BEFORE:

To make the stew: Store the prepared seitan and cut-up carrots and celery in an airtight container in the fridge.

☀ IN THE MORNING:

Oil the crock of your slow cooker. Combine all the stew ingredients in the slow cooker. Add more water if you will cook it longer than 8 hours, or if your slow cooker runs a little hot. Cook on low for 6 to 8 hours. Remove the bay leaf and thyme and rosemary sprigs. Taste and adjust the seasonings.

To make the dumplings: About 40 minutes before serving, combine all the dumpling ingredients in a bowl and work until it comes together into a dough. Turn the mixture out onto a floured cutting board and roll to the thickness of a thick pie crust. Cut into rectangles and place in the slow cooker. Stir to incorporate the dumplings, turn up the slow cooker to high, and cook for 30 minutes more. The dough will thicken up as it cooks. Add more broth if needed.

YIELD: 4 to 6 servings
TOTAL PREP TIME: 30 minutes
TOTAL COOKING TIME: 6 to 8 hours plus 40 minutes to cook the dumplings

FROM-THE-PANTRY POT PIE

This recipe is a great way to use up what you have on hand.
You can also incorporate leftover veggies, sausage, or beans.

FOR THE STEW:

1 small onion, minced (optional)

2 cloves garlic, minced (optional)

1 large stalk celery, minced (optional)

1½ cups (340 g) cubed chicken-flavored seitan, store-bought or homemade (page 21), crumbled cooked sausage, diced tofu, beans, or diced potato

1 pound (454 g) frozen mixed green beans, corn, carrots, and peas (you can use fresh or leftovers instead)

1 cup (235 ml) water, plus more if needed

2 tablespoons (12 g) vegan chicken-flavored bouillon or 4 tablespoons (24 g) Chickeny Bouillon (page 19)

1 teaspoon dried thyme

Salt and pepper, to taste

2 tablespoons (16 g) flour, if needed

FOR THE BISCUITS:

1 cup (120 g) white, whole wheat, or gluten-free flour

½ teaspoon salt

½ teaspoon thyme (optional)

1½ teaspoons baking powder

3 tablespoons (45 ml) olive oil

½ cup (120 ml) plain or unsweetened nondairy milk

☾ THE NIGHT BEFORE:

To make the stew: Place the cut-up onion, garlic, celery, and seitan in a large airtight container and store in the refrigerator.

☀ IN THE MORNING:

Oil the crock of your slow cooker. Combine all of the ingredients except the flour in the slow cooker. Add 1 to 2 cups (235 to 470 ml) extra water if you will cook it longer than 8 hours, or if your slow cooker runs a little hot. Cook on low for 6 to 8 hours.

About 30 minutes before serving, add more water if the mixture is too thick, or add the flour if the stew needs to thicken up a bit. Taste and adjust the seasonings.

To make the biscuits: Combine all the biscuit ingredients in a bowl and work until it comes together into a dough. Turn the mixture out onto a floured cutting board, roll out about ½ inch (1.3 cm) thick, and cut into circles with the rim of a glass. Place in the slow cooker on top of the filling. Turn up the slow cooker to high. Prop open the lid with the handle of a wooden spoon, or place a clean dishtowel under the lid to prevent condensation from dripping onto your biscuits. Cook an additional 30 minutes.

YIELD: 4 to 6 servings
TOTAL PREP TIME: 30 minutes
TOTAL COOKING TIME: 6 to 8 hours plus 30 minutes to cook the biscuits

RECIPE IDEAS & VARIATIONS

Make biscuits days ahead and freeze. It will take about 15 more minutes for them to cook, but you won't have to bother with making them when you get home. Plus, it never hurts to have ready-to-bake biscuits in the freezer for a last-minute treat.

CHILI RELLENO CASSEROLE

▶ GLUTEN-FREE*

This dish is an almost soufflé that's light and flavored with cumin and chili powder and has a cheesy poblano filling. The batter will seem quite thick, but don't worry—it comes out fine.

INGREDIENTS:

3 poblanos, halved, seeds and stems removed

1 package (15 ounces, or 420 g) tofu (silken, soft, or firm will all work)

¾ cup (175 ml) plain or unsweetened nondairy milk

½ cup (70 g) cornmeal

½ cup (48 g) nutritional yeast (*use gluten-free)

¼ cup (31 g) chickpea flour

1 teaspoon cumin

1 teaspoon chili powder

1 teaspoon salt

½ teaspoon garlic powder

¼ teaspoon turmeric

½ teaspoon baking powder

1 teaspoon baking soda

1 cup (115 g) shredded vegan cheese (I used Daiya mozzarella because it looks like queso fresco)

☾ THE NIGHT BEFORE:

Preheat the broiler in the oven. Put the 6 halves of the poblanos on an oiled baking sheet, place on the top rack, and broil until the skins blister but do not let burn. It's a small window, so check every 4 or 5 minutes. Let them sit until they are cool enough to handle but still warm, and then peel the skins off. Store in an airtight container in the fridge.

About 2 hours before serving: Put the tofu in a blender or food processor with the nondairy milk and process until smooth. In a large mixing bowl (or mixer), combine the cornmeal, nutritional yeast, chickpea flour, spices, baking powder, and baking soda. Mix well, then add the tofu mixture and stir to combine.

☀ IN THE MORNING:

Oil the crock of your slow cooker and spread half the mixture on the bottom. Arrange the roasted poblanos on top, sprinkle on the shredded cheese, and then spread the remaining half of the mixture on top. Cook on high for 1½ to 2 hours, or until it sets up. The middle will still be a little jiggly, but it will firm up as it cools. Let sit for 10 to 15 minutes before serving.

YIELD: 4 servings
TOTAL PREP TIME: 40 minutes
TOTAL COOKING TIME: 1½ to 2 hours

RECIPE IDEAS & VARIATIONS

Try adding additional sauteed veggies into the poblano layer.

SERVING SUGGESTION

This is a very rich casserole, so serve with a large salad to balance the meal.

CHORIZO AND SWEET POTATO ENCHILADA CASSEROLE

This is a very easy dish that has a more complex taste because of the combination of spicy chorizo and sweet potatoes. You can use your favorite canned or homemade enchilada sauce. I like to make this on a Saturday when I'm in the kitchen making staples for the month (bouillon, seitan, sausage, etc.). Then it's ready right when I need to eat!

INGREDIENTS:

1 medium-size sweet potato, thinly sliced

2 to 3 cups (470 to 705 ml) enchilada sauce

1 package (11 ounces, or 308 g) corn tortillas

½ package (12 ounces, or 340 g) soy chorizo

1 can (15 ounces, or 420 g) black beans, drained and rinsed, or 1½ cups (340 g) homemade (page 17)

RECIPE IDEAS & VARIATIONS

Make a gluten-free version by using crumbled tofu in place of the chorizo. Use beans instead to make it a soy-free dish.

☾ THE NIGHT BEFORE:

Store the sliced sweet potato in an airtight container in the fridge.

☼ IN THE MORNING:

Oil the crock of your slow cooker and pour one-fourth of the sauce over the bottom. Cover the sauce with a single layer of tortillas and top with one-third of the chorizo, one-third of the sweet potatoes, and one-third of the black beans. Top with another one-fourth of the sauce. Repeat the layering (starting with the tortillas) two more times, cover with a final layer of corn tortillas, and spread the remaining sauce on top. Cook on low for 4 to 5 hours, or on high for 2 to 3 hours. If your slow cooker runs hot, pour on a little extra sauce to keep it from drying out.

YIELD: 6 servings
TOTAL PREP TIME: 15 minutes
TOTAL COOKING TIME: 4 to 5 hours on low or 2 to 3 hours on high

CHICK'N MUSHROOM CASSEROLE

This is a comforting retro casserole that you'll wish you had when you were growing up. The creamy cashew sour cream adds richness to the mushroom sauce, while the pasta and seitan make it hearty and filling. It's a perfect potluck dish, as well as a warming meal on a snowy day.

FOR THE CASHEW SOUR CREAM:

½ cup (73 g) cashews

½ cup (120 ml) water

2 teaspoons lemon juice

INGREDIENTS:

2 tablespoons (30 ml) olive oil

1 small onion, minced

2 cloves garlic, minced

1 package (10 ounces, or 280 g) sliced mushrooms

1 tablespoon (6 g) vegan chicken-flavored bouillon or 2 tablespoons (12 g) Chickeny Bouillon (page 19)

4 cups (940 ml) plain nondairy milk (unsweetened, if possible)

1½ cups (340 g) cubed chicken-flavored seitan, store-bought or homemade (page 21)

8 ounces (225 g) dried whole wheat pasta shells or rotini

½ teaspoon dried thyme

½ teaspoon dried marjoram

Salt and pepper, to taste

2 tablespoons (16 g) flour, if needed

Bread crumbs, for topping

☾ THE NIGHT BEFORE:

To make the cashew sour cream: In a food processor or blender combine the cashews, water, and lemon juice and process until smooth and creamy.

Heat the oil in a skillet over medium heat and sauté the onion until translucent, 3 to 5 minutes. Add the garlic and mushrooms and sauté until the mushrooms reduce in size and are tender, 5 to 10 minutes. Store the sautéed vegetables and the prepared sour cream in separate airtight containers in the fridge.

☼ IN THE MORNING:

About 1½ hours before serving: Oil the crock of your slow cooker. Combine the sautéed veggies, cashew sour cream, bouillon, milk, seitan, pasta, thyme, marjoram, and salt and pepper in the slow cooker. Mix thoroughly and cook on high for 1 to 1½ hours, or until the pasta is al dente.

If the pasta is ready but the sauce is not thick enough, add the flour and stir to combine. This should thicken up the mix. Top each serving with the bread crumbs.

YIELD: 4 servings
TOTAL PREP TIME: 15 minutes
TOTAL COOKING TIME: 1 to 1½ hours

SERVING SUGGESTIONS

Get nostalgic and top with your family's favorite casserole topping from your youth. Topping ideas include crushed potato chips or Ritz crackers, canned french fried onions, or just about anything crunchy, as long as it's vegan, of course!

ITALIAN EGGPLANT CASSEROLE WITH CASHEW-TOFU RICOTTA

▶ GLUTEN-FREE*

This is my healthy substitute for eggplant parmigiana. Not frying the eggplant saves time and calories, and both of those can be at a premium. It's very saucy and perfect over pasta.

FOR THE **CASHEW-TOFU RICOTTA:**

½ cup (68 g) cashews

½ cup (48 g) nutritional yeast (*use gluten-free)

3 cloves garlic

1 package (15 ounces, or 420 g) firm tofu

½ cup (120 ml) unsweetened nondairy milk

½ to 1 teaspoon salt (to taste)

Pepper, to taste

INGREDIENTS:

1 large eggplant, thinly sliced

1 jar (25 ounces, or 700 g) marinara sauce, store-bought or homemade (page 101)

Cooked pasta (*use gluten-free pasta), for serving

☾ THE NIGHT BEFORE:

To make the ricotta: In a food processor or blender, combine all the ricotta ingredients. Blend until smooth and creamy. Store the ricotta and the sliced eggplant in separate containers in the fridge.

☼ IN THE MORNING:

Oil the crock of your slow cooker and pour in one-third of the marinara sauce. Top with half of the eggplant, half of the ricotta, and another one-third of the sauce. Repeat the layers once more, then top with the remaining sauce. Cook on low for 6 to 8 hours. Serve over the pasta.

If your slow cooker does not run hot and the final product is too watery, prop up the lid on the handle of a wooden spoon and turn the slow cooker to high. In 30 minutes to 1 hour most of the water will evaporate.

YIELD: 8 servings
TOTAL PREP TIME: 15 minutes
TOTAL COOKING TIME: 6 to 8 hours

SERVING SUGGESTIONS

Meatless Sausage and Mushroom Ragu (page 103) and Make-Your-Own Marinara Sauce (page 101) are both great sauces to use with this dish.

BETTER-THAN-THE-CLASSIC SHEPHERD'S PIE

In this recipe, we add some celery root and parsnips to the usual potato mash.
It has the same whitish color, but has more flavor and a touch of sweetness.

INGREDIENTS:

1 package (8 ounces, or 225 g) tempeh, cut into chunks

2 tablespoons (30 ml) olive oil

1 small onion, minced

2 cloves garlic, minced

1½ cups (165 g) sausage crumbles or Apple Sage Sausage (page 23)

3 parsnips, peeled if not organic and cut into chunks

1 small celery root, peeled, roots trimmed, and cut into chunks

2 medium-size potatoes, peeled and cut into chunks

1 tablespoon (6 g) vegan chicken-flavored bouillon or 2 tablespoons (12 g) Chickeny Bouillon (page 19)

1 to 1½ cups (235 to 355 ml) water

1 teaspoon Cajun seasoning

Salt and pepper, to taste

2 to 4 tablespoons (28 to 56 g) nondairy butter

½ to 1 cup (120 to 235 ml) plain nondairy milk (unsweetened, if possible)

☾ THE NIGHT BEFORE:

Steam the tempeh in a steamer basket for 10 minutes. This takes out some of the bitterness. Heat the oil in a skillet over medium heat and sauté the onion until translucent, 3 to 5 minutes. Add the garlic and sauté for 1 minute longer. Add the steamed tempeh and break into crumbles with a spatula. If you are using a sausage that needs to be precooked (that's not already in crumbles), add it now and cook until done, 10 to 12 minutes. Cut up parsnips, potatoes, and celery root. Store the tempeh mixture and the cut-up parsnips, celery root, and potatoes in a large airtight container in the refrigerator.

☼ IN THE MORNING:

Oil the crock of your slow cooker. Combine the tempeh mixture, sausage, bouillon, 1 cup (235 ml) water, Cajun seasoning, and salt and pepper in the slow cooker. (If your slow cooker runs hot or you will be gone longer than 8 hours, add the extra ½ cup [120 ml] water.) Top with a piece of parchment paper or aluminium foil and place parsnips, celery root, and potatoes on top of it, so that they are separated from the stew. Cook on low for 6 to 8 hours.

About 30 minutes before serving, carefully remove the parsnips, celery root, and potatoes using tongs, and place in a large mixing bowl. Add the butter to taste and ½ cup (120 ml) milk, and mash or purée. Add the remaining ½ cup (120 ml) milk if the mixture is too dry. Season with salt and pepper to taste.

Stir the stew in the slow cooker, then top with the mashed potatoes. Turn up the slow cooker to high and cook until the potato mixture is piping hot, 20 to 40 minutes.

YIELD: 6 servings
TOTAL PREP TIME: 15 minutes
TOTAL COOKING TIME: 6 to 8 hours

ATOMIC TOFU PECAN LOAF

▶ GLUTEN-FREE*

This loaf was inspired by *Vegan Lunch Box*'s Magical Loaf Studio website.
I combined about four recipes and added a few things on top of that. You can
add almost anything you have on hand, so it's a great way to use up leftovers!

INGREDIENTS:

1 cup (235 ml) water

1 cup (96 g) textured vegetable protein (tvp)

3 sun-dried tomatoes

1 cup (250 g) cubed silken, soft, or firm tofu

½ cup (55 g) pecans

1 cup (110 g) oat bran (*use gluten-free)

¼ cup (24 g) nutritional yeast

1 teaspoon garlic powder

1 teaspoon onion salt or ½ teaspoon plain salt

1 tablespoon (3 g) Italian seasoning

½ teaspoon liquid smoke

½ teaspoon garlic hot pepper sauce (optional)

Pepper, to taste

¼ cup (60 ml) ketchup

¼ cup (60 ml) A1 steak sauce

2 tablespoons (30 ml) vegan Worcestershire sauce
   (*use gluten-free)

☾ THE NIGHT BEFORE:

Boil the water in a saucepan, mix in the tvp, remove from the heat, and set aside for about 10 minutes while it reconstitutes. If you are using sun-dried tomatoes that are not packed in oil, soften them with the tvp in the hot water.

In a food processor, combine the tofu, pecans, and sun-dried tomatoes until minced.

Combine the tofu mixture, oat bran, nutritional yeast, garlic powder, onion salt, Italian seasoning, liquid smoke, hot pepper sauce, and pepper in a large mixing bowl. Add the reconstituted tvp and mix thoroughly. In a separate small bowl, combine the ketchup, steak sauce, and Worcestershire and set aside. Cover and refrigerate both.

☀ IN THE MORNING:

Oil the crock of your slow cooker. Pat the loaf mixture into the slow cooker. Cook on low for 6 to 8 hours.

About 30 minutes before serving, spread the ketchup mixture over the top of the loaf.

YIELD: 6 servings
TOTAL PREP TIME: 30 minutes
TOTAL COOKING TIME: 6 to 8 hours

RECIPE IDEAS & VARIATIONS

Substitute ½ small onion and 2 cloves garlic, minced and sautéed in oil for garlic powder.

SERVING SUGGESTION

Serve with mashed potatoes and mushroom gravy, green beans cooked with liquid smoke, and carrots.

CORN-TASTIC TEX-MEX LOAF

Many times I end up with half a package of chorizo and a few corn tortillas. Making a loaf out of the ingredients seemed like the best solution, and you can add bits and pieces of whatever you have on hand. You get the flavors of the chorizo combined with a cheesy corn taste in one bite. It's perfect to serve with Spanish Quinoa (page 107).

INGREDIENTS:

3 corn tortillas

½ package (12 ounces, or 340 g) vegan chorizo

½ cup (70 g) cornmeal

½ cup (48 g) nutritional yeast

3 tablespoons (21 g) ground flaxseed mixed with ¼ cup (60 ml) water

1 package (12 ounces, or 340 g) silken, soft, or firm tofu

Juice of 1 lime

¼ to ½ teaspoon hot pepper sauce (to taste)

½ teaspoon garlic powder

½ teaspoon chili powder

¼ to ½ teaspoon salt (to taste)

☾ THE NIGHT BEFORE:

Grind the corn tortillas in a food processor, then put the contents in a large bowl, add the chorizo and cornmeal, and stir to combine. Combine the nutritional yeast, flaxseed mixture, tofu, lime juice, hot sauce, garlic powder, chili powder, and salt in a blender or food processor and purée. Add the tofu mixture to the chorizo mixture and stir to combine thoroughly. Store in an airtight container in the fridge.

☀ IN THE MORNING:

Oil the crock of your slow cooker. Pat the loaf mixture into the slow cooker. Cook on low for 6 to 8 hours. Prop open the lid with a wooden spoon handle or put a clean dish towel underneath the lid to prevent the condensation from dripping onto the loaf during cooking.

YIELD: 6 servings
TOTAL PREP TIME: 30 minutes
TOTAL COOKING TIME: 6 to 8 hours

RECIPE IDEAS & VARIATIONS

You can use more or fewer corn tortillas depending on what you have an hand. Just adjust the cornmeal accordingly.

HOLIDAY TEMPEH AND SAGE LOAF

▶ GLUTEN-FREE*

This loaf reminds me a little of Thanksgiving, and in fact I may just serve it as my main course this year. Leftovers make great sandwiches with cranberry sauce.

INGREDIENTS:

1 packages (8 ounces, or 225 g) tempeh (*use plain soy tempeh), cubed

1 small onion

2 cloves garlic

2 stalks celery

1 medium-size carrot

1 cup (70 g) sliced mushrooms

2 tablespoons (30 ml) olive oil

1 cup (115 g) whole wheat bread crumbs (*use gluten-free bread crumbs)

2 tablespoons (14 g) ground flaxseed mixed with 2 tablespoons (30 ml) warm water

2 tablespoons (12 g) vegan chicken-flavored bouillon or 4 tablespoons (24 g) Chickeny Bouillon (page 19)

1 teaspoon thyme

1 teaspoon rubbed sage

½ teaspoon oregano

½ teaspoon dried rosemary or ¼ teaspoon ground

½ teaspoon salt

☾ THE NIGHT BEFORE:

Steam the tempeh in a steamer basket for 10 minutes. This takes out some of the bitterness. While the temeph is cooking, use a food processor to mince the onion, garlic, celery, carrot, and mushrooms. Pulse until you have tiny pieces of veggies, but not so much that it liquefies. Heat the oil in a skillet over medium heat and sauté the veggies until the onion is translucent, about 3 minutes. Crumble the cooked tempeh into a large bowl, then add the sautéed veggies, bread crumbs, flaxseed mixture, bouillon, thyme, sage, oregano, rosemary, and salt. Store in an airtight container in the refrigerator.

☀ IN THE MORNING:

Oil the crock of your slow cooker. Pat the loaf mixture into the slow cooker. Cook on low for 6 to 8 hours. Prop open the lid with a wooden spoon handle or put a clean dish towel underneath the lid to prevent the condensation from dripping onto the loaf during cooking.

YIELD: 6 servings
TOTAL PREP TIME: 30 minutes
TOTAL COOKING TIME: 6 to 8 hours

CHAPTER 6

EASY-TO-MAKE PASTA AND GRAIN DISHES

Pasta and grains are the staples of any diet, but they seem to play an even bigger part in the life of a vegan. In this chapter you'll get a few pasta sauces, too. Sauces are another great addition to a weekend cooking rotation. They freeze well and can be used in other recipes.

Pasta can be dressed up in lasagna, which is a perfect dish for introducing nonvegans to vegan food. And people who say they can't be a vegan because they'll miss cheese too much can be introduced to vegan cheesy options in the Smoky Mac and Cheese (page 115) or Cheesy Broccoli Rice (page 113).

You saw in chapter 2 that you can make plain rice in the slow cooker, and it's in this chapter that you can really appreciate it. Jambalaya is my favorite dish to bring to a potluck. You cook everything but the rice all day, then add the rice an hour before you want to eat. Quinoa is a perfect grain to cook in the slow cooker as well, and if you haven't tried it before, Spanish Quinoa (page 107) will introduce you to this nutritious and versatile grain.

With all the grain dishes and non-lasagna pastas you will need to stir more frequently, which helps the dish cook more evenly, plus it just feels good to break the old don't-lift-your-slow-cooker-lid rule.

1. Make-Your-Own Marinara Sauce
2. Meatless Sausage and Mushroom Ragu
3. Pumpkin and White Bean Lasagna
4. Mushroom Lasagna with Garlic-Tofu Sauce
5. Spanish Quinoa
6. Mix-and-Match Jambalaya
7. Basic Fuss-Free Risotto
8. Creamy Butternut Squash Risotto
9. Cheesy Broccoli Rice
10. Smoky Mac and Cheese

MAKE-YOUR-OWN MARINARA SAUCE

▶ SOY-FREE ▶ GLUTEN-FREE

Sooner or later you'll find yourself wishing you had some marinara sauce on hand.
Why not make a big pot of it now and freeze some for later? You can add your
favorite veggies, wine, or sun-dried tomatoes and make it just the way you like it.

....

INGREDIENTS:

1 teaspoon olive oil

1 large onion, minced

3 cloves garlic, minced

2 cans (28 ounces, or 784 g each) crushed or diced
tomatoes or 6 cups (1360 g) Preserve-the-Harvest
Diced Tomatoes (page 25)

1 tablespoon (15 ml) agave nectar or (13 g) sugar

1 teaspoon dried basil

1 teaspoon dried oregano

½ teaspoon dried thyme

¼ teaspoon dried rosemary

Salt and pepper, to taste

☾ THE NIGHT BEFORE:

Heat the oil in a skillet over medium heat and sauté the
onion until translucent, 3 to 5 minutes. Add the garlic and
sauté for 2 minutes longer. Store in an airtight container
in the refrigerator.

☼ IN THE MORNING:

Combine all the ingredients in your slow cooker. Be sure to
adjust the salt if you are using canned tomatoes, because
they may already contain salt. Cook on low for 6 to 8 hours.
About 10 to 15 minutes before serving, add water if needed.
Taste and adjust the seasonings.

Freeze the extra in ice cube trays, resealable plastic bags,
or freezer containers.

YIELD: 8 servings
TOTAL PREP TIME: 15 minutes
TOTAL COOKING TIME: 6 to 8 hours

RECIPE IDEAS & VARIATIONS

Mix and match herbs to suit your taste. If you are
using canned tomatoes, take advantage of some of
the ones that already have roasted garlic and herbs in
them. Just be sure to adjust the seasonings you add.

MEATLESS SAUSAGE AND MUSHROOM RAGU

This is definitely not the ragu from your supermarket shelves! It's a great way to transition hard-core meat eaters to a meatless meal and makes the perfect topping for grilled polenta. You can just buy a premade tube of polenta and slice it, then crisp it in the oven or on a grill.

INGREDIENTS:

1 teaspoon olive oil

1 medium-size onion, minced

3 cloves garlic, minced

1 package (14 ounces, or 392 g) vegan sausage, store-bought or homemade (page 23), sliced into rounds

2 cans (28 ounces, or 784 g each) crushed tomatoes

1 pound (454 g) crimini or button mushrooms, chopped

2 large portobello mushrooms, chopped

Freshly ground black pepper, to taste

1 tablespoon (15 ml) balsamic vinegar

2 to 3 tablespoons (30 to 45 ml) red or port wine

2 tablespoons (5 g) chopped fresh basil

☾ THE NIGHT BEFORE:

Heat the oil in a skillet over medium heat and sauté the onion until translucent, 3 to 5 minutes. Add the garlic and sauté for 1 minute longer. Transfer to a large airtight container. In the same skillet that you cooked the onions, cook the sausage until brown, 5 to 10 minutes. Break the patties apart with the spatula to make crumbles. Transfer to the same bowl as the onions and store in the fridge.

☼ IN THE MORNING:

Combine the sautéed onion, sausage, tomatoes, mushrooms, pepper, vinegar, and wine in the slow cooker. Cook on low for 6 to 8 hours. About 10 minutes before serving, add water if needed, extra seasoning, and the basil.

YIELD: 12 servings
TOTAL PREP TIME: 20 minutes
TOTAL COOKING TIME: 6 to 8 hours

RECIPE IDEAS & VARIATIONS

- This recipe makes enough to feed a dinner party and still have leftovers, but it freezes well. Freeze in ice cube trays, then once the cubes are frozen solid, pop them out into a resealable plastic bag. This way you can defrost exactly the amount you need, even if you want a single-serving size.

- Cut this recipe in half if you are using a 3½ quart (3.3 L) slow cooker.

PUMPKIN AND WHITE BEAN LASAGNA

This is a perfect dish for introducing nonvegans to vegan food and is much healthier than the traditional, fat-laden lasagna. It's easy to make and hearty. Add a nice spinach salad with a balsamic vinaigrette, and you're all ready to have friends over for dinner.

....

FOR THE PUMPKIN–TOFU RICOTTA:

1 tablespoon (15 ml) olive oil

3 sun-dried tomatoes, rehydrated (pour boiling water over them and let them sit for 5 minutes)

1 package (15 ounces, or 420 g) silken, soft, or firm tofu

1 can (15 ounces, or 420 g) cooked pumpkin or 1½ cups (368 g) puréed cooked fresh

¼ cup (24 g) nutritional yeast

1 tablespoon (3 g) Italian seasoning

1 teaspoon onion powder

2 cloves garlic, crushed

Salt and pepper, to taste

FOR THE LASAGNA:

1 jar (24 ounces, or 672 g) marinara sauce, store-bought or homemade (page 101)

About ¾ package (10 ounces, or 280 g) whole wheat lasagne noodles (the regular kind, not the no-boil noodles)

1 can (14½ ounces, or 406 g) white beans, drained and rinsed, or 1½ cups (340 g) homemade (page 17)

☾ THE NIGHT BEFORE:

To make the pumpkin–tofu ricotta: In a food processor, blend the olive oil and the rehydrated sun-dried tomatoes until a paste forms. There may still be some lumps. Add the remaining ricotta ingredients and blend until creamy. Add a little water if the mixture is too thick. Taste and adjust the seasonings. Store in an airtight container in the fridge.

☼ IN THE MORNING:

To make the lasagna: Spray the crock with olive oil so you won't have a nightmare cleanup on your hands later on.

Spread a thin layer of sauce over the bottom of the slow cooker. Break off the corners on one side of each noodle so they fit snugly in the slow cooker. You can add the corners in as well. Place a single layer of noodles over the sauce. Spread one-third of the ricotta mixture over the noodles. Spread another thin layer of sauce over the ricotta and sprinkle one-third of the white beans on top of that. Repeat the layers two more times, ending with a last layer of lasagne noodles, and then top that with more sauce.

Cook on low for 3 to 4 hours or on high for 1½ to 2 hours, until a fork will easily go through the middle and the pasta is al dente. Add ½ cup (120 ml) extra sauce or water if you need to leave it an hour or two longer.

YIELD: 6 servings
TOTAL PREP TIME: 20 minutes
TOTAL COOKING TIME: 3 to 4 hours on low or 1½ to 2 hours on high

MUSHROOM LASAGNA WITH GARLIC-TOFU SAUCE

This is a quick and easy dish that is elegant and perfect for last-minute company.
For a special treat add a layer of chantrelle or lobster mushrooms and use
one-third less of the regular mushrooms that are called for in the recipe.

FOR THE BECHAMEL SAUCE:

1 package (15 ounces, or 420 g) silken or soft tofu

Juice of 1/2 lemon

1 cup (235 ml) water

3 cloves garlic or 1 teaspoon dried

1/2 to 1 teaspoon salt (to taste)

1 1/2 tablespoons (9 g) vegan chicken-flavored bouillon
  or 3 tablespoons (18 g) Chickeny Bouillon (page 19)

1/4 cup (24 g) nutritional yeast

INGREDIENTS:

2 tablespoons (30 ml) olive oil

20 ounces (560 g) mushrooms, sliced

2 sprigs rosemary

1/2 to 3/4 package (10 ounces, or 280 g) whole wheat
  lasagne noodles (the regular kind, not the no boil
  noodles)

RECIPE IDEAS & VARIATIONS

Not fond of mushrooms? Substitute precooked vegan
beef or sausage crumbles instead.

☪ THE NIGHT BEFORE:

To make the bechamel sauce: Pureé all the sauce ingredients in a food processor or blender until smooth.

Heat the oil in a skillet over medium heat and sauté the
mushrooms with the rosemary until they give off their
water and begin to brown, about 10 minutes. Remove and
discard the rosemary sprigs. Store the sauce and mushrooms in separate airtight containers in the fridge.

☀ IN THE MORNING:

Oil the crock of the slow cooker and spread one-fifth of
the sauce on the bottom, then top with a layer of lasagne
noodles. Break off the corners on one side of each noodle
so they fit snugly in the slow cooker. You can add the
corners in as well. Place a layer of noodles over the sauce.
Add a layer of one-third of the mushrooms and top with
another one-fifth of the sauce. Repeat the layers two more
times, ending with a last layer of lasagne noodles, and
then top that with the remaining sauce.

Cook on high for 1 1/2 to 2 1/2 hours, until a fork will easily
go through the middle and the pasta is al dente.

YIELD: 4 servings
TOTAL PREP TIME: 20 minutes
TOTAL COOKING TIME: 1 1/2 to 2 1/2 hours

SPANISH QUINOA

▸ SOY-FREE ▸ GLUTEN-FREE

Spanish rice was one of my favorite side dishes growing up. This recipe uses quinoa instead of rice. It's a nice change of pace and just as tasty.

INGREDIENTS:

2 tablespoons (30 ml) olive oil

1 small onion, chopped

2 cloves garlic, minced

1 bell pepper, cored and chopped

3 cups (705 g) water

1½ cups (260 g) quinoa

2 tablespoons (12 g) vegan chicken-flavored bouillon or 4 tablespoons (24 g) Chickeny Bouillon (page 19)

2 tablespoons (32 g) tomato paste

1 teaspoon salt

½ teaspoon chili powder

DIRECTIONS:

Heat the oil in a skillet over medium heat and sauté the onion until translucent, 3 to 5 minutes. Add the garlic and bell pepper and sauté until the pepper is soft, 3 to 5 minutes.

Combine the sautéed veggies, water, quinoa, bouillon, tomato paste, salt, and chili powder in the slow cooker. Stir until the tomato paste and bouillon are mixed in the liquid. Cook on high for 1½ to 2 hours, until the quinoa has unfurled. Taste and adjust the seasonings.

YIELD: 8 servings
TOTAL PREP TIME: 15 minutes
TOTAL COOKING TIME: 1½ to 2 hours

RECIPE IDEAS & VARIATIONS

Add a can of black beans or some chicken-flavored seitan, store-bought or homemade (page 21), to make this a one-dish meal.

MIX-AND-MATCH JAMBALAYA

Vegans and meat eaters alike love jambalaya. It's an easy dish to make for a dinner party, and it's filling to boot. You can mix and match the proteins to your preference or to use what you have on hand. I like to use Italian sausage and chicken-flavored seitan, but you can use tempeh, tofu, or even red beans as the center attraction if you want. I usually use white jasmine rice, but any rice will work. Brown rice will require a little more cooking time, but it adds tons of nutrients.

INGREDIENTS:

1 tablespoon (15 ml) olive oil

1 medium-size onion, minced

2 cloves garlic, minced

2 or 3 large vegan Italian sausage links, cut into half-moons, or steamed tempeh cubes

1 to 2 cups (225 to 450 g) cubed chicken-flavored seitan, store-bought or homemade (page 21), or cubed firm tofu marinated in 2 tablespoons (12 g) vegan chicken-flavored bouillon, or 4 tablespoons (24 g) Chickeny Bouillon (page 19) and 1 cup (235 ml) water

1 green bell pepper, cored and chopped

1 red or orange bell pepper, cored and chopped

1 can (14½ ounces, or 406 g) diced tomatoes or 1½ cups (340 g) Preserve-the-Harvest Diced Tomatoes (page 25)

1 teaspoon to 1 tablespoon hot pepper sauce (to taste)

2 teaspoons Cajun seasoning

½ teaspoon liquid smoke or smoked paprika

¼ to 1 teaspoon red pepper flakes or chipotle chile powder (to taste)

3 cups (705 ml) water, plus more as needed

2 tablespoons (12 g) vegan chicken-flavored bouillon or 4 tablespoons (24 g) Chickeny Bouillon (page 19)

Salt and pepper, to taste

1½ cups (293 g) uncooked rice

☪ THE NIGHT BEFORE:

Heat the oil in a skillet over medium heat and sauté the onion until translucent, 3 to 5 minutes. Add the garlic and sauté for 1 minute longer. Combine the sautéed onion and cut-up sausage, tofu, and bell peppers in a large airtight container and store in the refrigerator.

☼ IN THE MORNING:

Combine the sautéed onion, sausage, seitan or tofu, bell peppers, tomatoes, hot sauce, Cajun seasoning, paprika, red pepper flakes, water, bouillon, and salt and pepper in the slow cooker. Cook on low for 6 to 8 hours.

About 1 hour before serving, add the rice. If the mixture looks dry, add 1 to 2 cups (235 to 470 ml) extra water. Turn up the slow cooker to high and cook for 45 minutes to 1 hour longer. Check occasionally to make sure it doesn't overcook. Taste and adjust the seasonings.

YIELD: 8 servings
TOTAL PREP TIME: 15 minutes
TOTAL COOKING TIME: 7 to 9 hours

BASIC FUSS-FREE RISOTTO

▸ SOY-FREE   ▸ GLUTEN-FREE

Risotto can be used as a base to show off fresh, sautéed, or steamed seasonal herbs and veggies. This is a dish that you can make on a weeknight after you come home from work because it only takes 1½ to 2½ hours to cook in the slow cooker. There's almost no stirring compared to the stove-top version, so you can even relax while it's cooking!

INGREDIENTS:

3 cups (705 ml) water

1½ cups (280 g) Arborio rice

2 cloves garlic, minced

2 tablespoons (12 g) vegan chicken-flavored bouillon or 4 tablespoons (24 g) Chickeny Bouillon (page 19)

Salt and pepper, to taste

DIRECTIONS:

Add the water, rice, garlic, and bouillon to the slow cooker. Cook on high for 1½ to 2½ hours, until the rice is cooked through but still al dente. Stir every 30 minutes and add extra water if needed. Season with salt and pepper to taste.

Serve topped with assorted seasonal sautéed or steamed veggies.

YIELD: 6 servings
TOTAL PREP TIME: 5 minutes
TOTAL COOKING TIME: 1½ to 2½ hours

SERVING SUGGESTION

For a stunning dish, steam some purple and orange cauliflower florets. Serve on top of the rissoto for a burst of color. You can also add some rainbow chard. Cut the colorful stems small and sauté them.

CREAMY BUTTERNUT SQUASH RISOTTO

▸ SOY-FREE ▸ GLUTEN-FREE*

Butternut squash makes the perfect fall risotto. I like to use a combination of herbs in this dish, but you can always just use one if you'd prefer. You can switch out any winter squash for the butternut depending on what you happen to have on hand.

INGREDIENTS:

2½ cups (588 ml) water

1½ cups (280 g) Arborio rice

1 can (15 ounces, or 420 g) cooked butternut squash or 1½ cups (368) pureéd cooked fresh

½ cup (48 g) nutritional yeast (*use gluten-free)

1 teaspoon thyme

¼ teaspoon rubbed sage

⅛ teaspoon dried rosemary

Salt and pepper, to taste

DIRECTIONS:

Add the water, rice, squash, nutritional yeast, thyme, sage, and rosemary to the slow cooker. Cook on high for 1½ to 2½ hours, until the rice is cooked through but still al dente. Stir every 20 to 30 minutes, adding extra water if needed. Season with salt and pepper and taste and adjust the herbs.

YIELD: 6 servings
TOTAL PREP TIME: 15 minutes
TOTAL COOKING TIME: 1½ to 2½ hours

DID YOU KNOW?

You can precook the squash in your slow cooker following the directions in Perfect Pumpkin Purée (page 34).

CHEESY BROCCOLI RICE

▸ SOY-FREE ▸ GLUTEN-FREE*

Cheesy rice was one of my favorite things to eat when
I was a kid. Later on, broccoli became a favorite addition.

INGREDIENTS:

3 cups (705 ml) water

1½ cups (280 g) long-grain brown rice

3 tablespoons (18 g) vegan chicken-flavored bouillon
    or 6 tablespoons (36 g) Chickeny Bouillon (page 19)

½ cup (48 g) nutritional yeast (*use gluten-free)

1 pound (454 g) fresh or frozen broccoli

Salt and pepper, to taste

1 cup (115 g) shredded vegan cheddar cheese (optional)

DIRECTIONS:

Add the water, rice, bouillon, and nutritional yeast to the
slow cooker. Cook on high for 1½ hours. Stir in the broccoli. Check every 10 to 15 minutes, adding more water if
needed, and stir the mixture until the rice and broccoli are
tender when pierced with a fork, 15 to 40 minutes, depending on whether you use fresh or frozen broccoli. If you
know you will be in a hurry you can defrost the broccoli in
the fridge the night before.

Once the rice is ready, add the salt and pepper to taste
and stir in the cheese.

YIELD: 6 servings
TOTAL PREP TIME: 5 minutes
TOTAL COOKING TIME: 2½ to 3 hours

SERVING SUGGESTION

This is a great side dish or a light main course if you
add some tofu or seitan.

SMOKY MAC AND CHEESE

Veganized comfort food is a beautiful thing. The liquid smoke and Cajun seasoning dress this dish up a little, but go ahead and leave them out if you're craving the kind of mac and cheese that you grew up on. This one is extra creamy, and leftovers reheat well.

....

INGREDIENTS:

4 cups (940 ml) nondairy milk

2 tablespoons (12 g) vegan chicken-flavored bouillon or 4 tablespoons (24 g) Chickeny Bouillon (page 19)

8 ounces (225 g) dried whole wheat macaroni

2 cups (230 g) shredded vegan cheddar cheese

1 cup (115 g) shredded vegan mozzarella cheese

¼ to ½ teaspoon liquid smoke (optional)

½ teaspoon Cajun seasoning (optional)

Salt and pepper, to taste

DIRECTIONS:

Oil the crock of your slow cooker. Toss all the ingredients into the slow cooker and stir to combine. Cook on high for 1 to 1½ hours, or until the pasta is al dente. You will get better results if you stir the mixture every 20 to 30 minutes. If you don't use whole wheat pasta it will cook faster, so check it around 45 minutes. It's important to check this one frequently or you will end up with mushy pasta.

YIELD: 4 servings
TOTAL PREP TIME: 10 minutes
TOTAL COOKING TIME: 1 to 1½ hours

RECIPE IDEAS & VARIATIONS

This is a great dish to sneak in a few veggies. Add leftover precooked vegetables to the slow cooker during the last 30 minutes of cooking.

CHAPTER 7

MOUTHWATERING MEATLESS MAINS

There's nothing more satisfying than coming home to food you have been craving. If you don't live in a large metropolitan area it can be hard to find vegan restaurants. With this chapter you can make your own Chinese takeout and a few upscale main courses for special dinners at a fraction of the price of going out to eat.

If you don't live in a vegan household you may get complaints about too many nights of vegetable stews over rice. The recipes in this chapter are hearty enough to satisfy even a nonvegan. Plus, sometimes vegans just need some stick-to-your-ribs meals, too. There are old-time comfort foods, such as Hearty Faux Steak and Gravy (page 126), as well as fancier dishes, including Tempeh Braised with Figs and Port Wine (page 123).

1. Kung Pao Chick'n
2. Sweet and Sour Smoked Tofu
3. Ma Po Tofu
4. Tempeh and Veggies in Spicy Peanut Sauce
5. Tempeh Braised with Figs and Port Wine
6. Chick'n Cacciatore
7. Braised Chick'n and Olives
8. Hearty Faux Steak and Gravy
9. Chick'n Normandy with Apples and Brandy Sauce
10. Chick'n Marsala

KUNG PAO CHICK'N

This spicy seitan dish gets a rich flavor from the mushrooms and
rice vinegar as well as a great crunch from the water chestnuts.

FOR THE SAUCE:

3 cloves garlic, minced

1 tablespoon (8 g) grated ginger

1½ cups (355 ml) water

¼ cup (60 ml) soy sauce

¼ cup (60 ml) seasoned rice vinegar or plain rice
vinegar mixed with 1 teaspoon sweetener

2 tablespoons (12 g) vegan chicken-flavored bouillon
or 4 tablespoons (24 g) Chickeny Bouillon (page 19)

¼ to ½ teaspoon red pepper flakes or sriracha (to taste)

INGREDIENTS:

1 bell pepper, cored and diced

5 ounces (140 g) mushrooms, diced

1 can (8 ounces, or 225 g) water chestnuts, drained
and diced

1 package (12 ounces, or 335 g) chicken-flavored
seitan, store-bought or homemade (page 21), diced

2 to 3 tablespoons (16 to 24 g) cornstarch

2 tablespoons (30 ml) sesame oil

Steamed rice, for serving

Chopped peanuts, for serving

☾ THE NIGHT BEFORE:

To make the sauce: Combine all the sauce ingredients and
store in an airtight container in the fridge. Store the cut-up
bell pepper, mushrooms, water chestnuts, and seitan in an
airtight container in the fridge.

☀ IN THE MORNING:

Combine the sauce, pepper, mushrooms, water chestnuts, and seitan in the slow cooker. Cook on low for 6 to
8 hours.

About 30 minutes before serving, turn up slow cooker
to high. Make a thickener by mixing the cornstarch with
some of the sauce from the slow cooker in a small cup,
then add it back to the slow cooker. Right before serving,
stir in the sesame oil. Serve over steamed rice, and top
with the peanuts.

YIELD: 4 servings
TOTAL PREP TIME: 15 minutes
TOTAL COOKING TIME: 6 to 8 hours

RECIPE IDEAS & VARIATIONS

- Get in some extra veggies by adding diced zucchini, carrots, and celery about 30 minutes before
  serving.

- Make a gluten-free version using tempeh or tofu in
  place of the seitan. Be sure to use gluten-free soy
  sauce, too!

SWEET AND SOUR SMOKED TOFU

▶ GLUTEN-FREE*

This dish was inspired by a recipe for sweet and sour seitan on Learning Vegan's blog. Save some money and make your Chinese takeout at home. Plus, you know exactly what went in it.

INGREDIENTS:

1 can (20 ounces, or 560 g) pineapple in juice

2 tablespoons (30 ml) low-sodium soy sauce (*use gluten-free)

2 to 3 teaspoons grated fresh ginger

1 package (8 ounces, or 225 g) smoked tofu, cubed, or 1 recipe Tea-Scented Tofu (page 24) made with Lapsang Souchong black tea

1 medium onion, cut in half and thinly sliced

1 large bell pepper, thinly sliced

2 large carrots, sliced

1 medium-size head broccoli, cut into bite-size pieces

3 tablespoons (24 g) cornstarch

3 tablespoons (45 ml) cold water

☾ THE NIGHT BEFORE:

Open the pineapple can and drain the juice into a small bowl. Add the soy sauce and ginger to the juice to make the sauce. Store the sauce, pineapple chunks, and cut-up tofu, onion, pepper, carrots, and broccoli in an airtight container in the fridge.

☼ IN THE MORNING:

Combine the sauce, onion, carrots, and tofu in the slow cooker. Cook on low for 6 to 8 hours.

About 30 to 45 minutes before serving, turn up slow cooker to high and add the pepper, broccoli, and pineapple chunks. Make a thickener by mixing the cornstarch and water in a small cup, then add it to the slow cooker. It's ready when the sauce has thickened and the broccoli is tender.

YIELD: 4 servings
TOTAL PREP TIME: 15 minutes
TOTAL COOKING TIME: 6 to 8 hours

RECIPE IDEAS & VARIATIONS

If you don't have canned pineapple you can use fresh or frozen. You'll just need about 1 cup (235 ml) of juice to substitute for the pineapple juice used in the sauce. Apple juice would be my first choice, but orange juice would work, too. After all, you're just using it to put the sweet into the sweet and sour!

MA PO TOFU

This is one of my favorite Chinese dishes. You can make it as mild or spicy as you like it. Silken tofu has a custardlike texture and is the main focus of this dish. If you don't like that silky texture, feel free to use soft or firm tofu instead. You can usually find black bean garlic sauce in the international food aisle of most large grocery stores.

FOR THE SAUCE:

2 tablespoons (30 ml) soy sauce

2 tablespoons (30 ml) rice wine or apple cider vinegar

3 tablespoons (48 g) tomato paste

1½ tablespoons (24 g) black bean garlic sauce

1 to 2 teaspoons sriracha (to taste)

½ teaspoon red pepper flakes (optional)

3 cloves garlic, minced

2 to 3 teaspoons grated fresh ginger

1 teaspoon agave nectar

1 cup (235 ml) water

¼ cup (60 ml) white wine

INGREDIENTS:

8 shiitake mushrooms, sliced

2 packages (12 ounces, or 336 g each) silken, soft, or firm tofu, cubed

3 tablespoons (24 g) cornstarch

1 medium-size head broccoli, cut into bite-size pieces (you can also use frozen)

1 tablespoon (15 ml) sesame oil

Steamed rice, for serving

☾ THE NIGHT BEFORE:

To make the sauce: Combine all the sauce ingredients and store in an airtight container in the refrigerator. Store the cut-up mushrooms, tofu, and broccoli in separate airtight containers in the refrigerator.

☀ IN THE MORNING:

Combine the sauce, mushrooms, and tofu in the slow cooker. Cook on low for 6 to 8 hours.

About 45 to 60 minutes before serving, turn up the slow cooker to high. Make a thickener by mixing the cornstarch with some of the sauce from the slow cooker in a small cup, then add it back to the slow cooker. When the sauce is thickened, add the broccoli and cook until bright green. Right before serving, stir in the sesame oil. Serve over steamed rice.

YIELD: 6 servings
TOTAL PREP TIME: 15 minutes
TOTAL COOKING TIME: 6 to 8 hours

A WORTHY NOTE

If you are planning on taking leftovers for lunch the next day, steam the broccoli separately so it does not overcook when you reheat it.

TEMPEH AND VEGGIES IN SPICY PEANUT SAUCE

▸ GLUTEN-FREE*

This is a great dish to make with veggies you already have on hand and need to use up. It's perfect for those days before payday when you need to eat out of the pantry, too.

....

INGREDIENTS:

1 package (8 ounces, or 225 g) tempeh (*use plain soy tempeh to make this dish gluten-free), cubed

Steamed rice, for serving

Lime wedges, for serving

Chopped cilantro, for serving

Chopped peanuts, for serving

FOR THE SAUCE:

1 cup (260 g) peanut butter

3 cloves garlic

3 to 4 cups (705 to 940 ml) water

1 tablespoon (6 g) vegan chicken-flavored bouillon or 2 tablespoons (12 g) Chickeny Bouillon (page 19)

Juice of 1/2 lime

1/2 teaspoon salt

1/2 teaspoon coriander

1/4 to 1/2 teaspoon hot chili powder (to taste)

1/3 teaspoon cardamom

1/4 teaspoon cumin

1 package (10 ounces, 280 g) frozen broccoli, thawed (or use fresh)

1 package (10 ounces, or 280 g) frozen green beans, thawed (or use fresh)

☾ THE NIGHT BEFORE:

Steam the tempeh in a steamer basket for 10 minutes. This takes out some of the bitterness.

To make the sauce: While the tempeh is cooking blend all the sauce ingredients in a blender or food processor. Use the larger amount of water if your slow cooker runs hot or if you will be away from home longer than 8 hours. If you are using frozen veggies put them in the fridge so they can defrost. Store the tempeh and sauce in an airtight container in the fridge.

☀ IN THE MORNING:

Oil the crock of your slow cooker. Add the tempeh and sauce and cook on low for 6 to 8 hours.

About 40 minutes before serving, add the broccoli and green beans and turn up the slow cooker to high. Add more water if needed, or if the sauce is too thin prop the lid up on the handle of a wooden spoon. It's ready when the veggies are perfectly cooked. Serve over rice, squeeze a lime wedge over, and top with the cilantro and peanuts.

YIELD: 6 servings
TOTAL PREP TIME: 15 minutes
TOTAL COOKING TIME: 6 to 8 hours

RECIPE IDEAS & VARIATIONS

Use fresh seasonal veggies instead of the broccoli and green beans. Add longer-cooking veggies such as carrots to the slow cooker in the morning.

TEMPEH BRAISED WITH FIGS AND PORT WINE

▸ GLUTEN-FREE*

Looking for a sophisticated dish? Well, look no further. This recipe combines the complex flavor of port wine with fresh figs and nutty tempeh. Serve over mashed potatoes with roasted asparagus for a meal that will wow the toughest critic.

INGREDIENTS:

2 tablespoons (30 ml) olive oil

1 small onion, minced

2 cloves garlic, minced

1 package (8 ounces, or 225 g) tempeh (*use plain soy tempeh to make this dish gluten-free), cubed

8 fresh figs, each cut into 6 wedges

½ cup (120 ml) water

1 cup (235 ml) port wine

1 tablespoon (15 ml) balsamic vinegar

1 tablespoon (6 g) vegan chicken-flavored bouillon or 2 tablespoons (12 g) Chickeny Bouillon (page 19)

1 sprig fresh rosemary

1 sprig fresh thyme

Salt and pepper, to taste

☾ THE NIGHT BEFORE:

Heat the oil in a skillet over medium heat and sauté the onion until translucent, 3 to 5 minutes. Add the garlic and sauté for 1 minute longer. Combine in an airtight container with the cut-up tempeh and figs and store in the fridge.

☀ IN THE MORNING:

Combine all the ingredients in the slow cooker. Cook on low for 6 to 8 hours.

YIELD: 4 servings
TOTAL PREP TIME: 10 minutes
TOTAL COOKING TIME: 6 to 8 hours

RECIPE IDEAS & VARIATIONS

You can use dried figs in place of fresh. The stew will be a bit sweeter—you may want to add another teaspoon of balsamic vinegar to balance.

CHICK'N CACCIATORE

▶ SOY-FREE

This is a nice way to dress up chicken-flavored meat substitutes,
and it works well for a causal dinner on the deck or a cozy dinner party.

INGREDIENTS:

2 tablespoons (30 ml) olive oil

1 small onion, chopped

2 cloves garlic, minced

1 package (8 ounces, or 225 g) sliced mushrooms

1 package (10½ ounces, or 300 g) chicken-flavored
seitan, store-bought or homemade (page 21), diced

1 can (14½ ounces, or 406 g) diced tomatoes or
1½ cups (340 g) Preserve-the-Harvest Diced
Tomatoes (page 25)

½ cup (120 ml) white wine or water

1½ tablespoons (9 g) vegan chicken-flavored bouillon
or 3 tablespoons (18 g) Chickeny Bouillon (page 19)

1 tablespoon (16 g) tomato paste

1 teaspoon dried basil

1 teaspoon dried oregano

1 sprig fresh rosemary or ½ teaspoon dried leaves
or ground

Salt and pepper, to taste

Cooked pasta, for serving

1 teaspoon chopped fresh basil, for serving

☾ THE NIGHT BEFORE:

Heat the oil in a skillet over medium heat and sauté the
onion until translucent, 3 to 5 minutes. Add the garlic and
mushrooms and sauté until the mushrooms give off their
water and begin to brown, about 10 minutes. Store the
sautéed mixture in an airtight container in the refrigerator.

☼ IN THE MORNING:

Oil the crock of your slow cooker. Combine the sautéed
vegetables, chicken seitan, tomatoes, wine, bouillon,
tomato paste, dried basil, oregano, rosemary, and salt and
pepper in the slow cooker. Cook on low for 6 to 8 hours.
Taste and adjust the seasonings. Serve over cooked pasta
and top with the fresh basil for an extra burst of flavor.

YIELD: 4 servings
TOTAL PREP TIME: 15 minutes
TOTAL COOKING TIME: 6 to 8 hours

SERVING SUGGESTION

Serve it by itself with a side salad and some steamed
veggies and you have a perfect light summer meal.

BRAISED CHICK'N AND OLIVES

Here's a perfect combo of salty olives and red wine
in a light tomato sauce that smothers the seitan.

INGREDIENTS:

1 stalk celery, minced

10 ounces (2,830 g) cherry tomatoes, cut in half,
or 1 can (14½ ounces, or 406 g) diced tomatoes

4 to 6 chicken-flavored seitan breasts, store-bought
or homemade (page 21)

1 cup (100 g) pitted and sliced olives mix

1 cup (235 ml) red wine

½ cup (120 ml) water

1 tablespoon (16 g) tomato paste

2 cloves garlic, minced

2 sprigs rosemary

Salt and pepper, to taste

☪ THE NIGHT BEFORE:

Store the cut-up celery and tomatoes in a large airtight
container in the refrigerator.

☀ IN THE MORNING:

Oil the crock of your slow cooker. Combine all the ingredients in the slow cooker. Cook on low for 6 to 8 hours.
Remove and discard the rosemary sprigs. Taste and adjust
the seasonings.

YIELD: 4 to 6 servings
TOTAL PREP TIME: 10 minutes
TOTAL COOKING TIME: 6 to 8 hours

A WORTHY NOTE

It's good anytime of the year, with fresh tomatoes in
the summer and canned tomatoes in the winter.

HEARTY FAUX STEAK AND GRAVY

▶ SOY-FREE

This is a heartwarming meal perfect for the end of a long workday. Add a salad, green beans, or steamed broccoli to make a traditional square meal.

....

FOR THE FAUX STEAK AND COATING:

2 tablespoons (30 ml) olive oil

½ cup (60 g) flour

½ teaspoon garlic powder

½ teaspoon marjoram

½ teaspoon basil

¼ teaspoon celery seed

¼ teaspoon pepper

Salt, to taste

4 steak-shaped pieces beef seitan, store-bought or homemade (page 22, chunks can be used in a pinch)

FOR THE COOKING BROTH AND GRAVY:

1 cup (235 ml) water (or broth from homemade seitan)

1½ tablespoons (9 g) vegan chicken-flavored bouillon or 3 tablespoons (18 g) Chickeny Bouillon (page 19) (if using water)

1 cup (235 ml) nondairy milk

3 to 5 tablespoons (24 to 40 g) flour

FOR THE POTATOES:

4 large baking potatoes, washed (leave peel on if desired)

½ cup (120 ml) nondairy milk

2 to 4 tablespoons (28 to 56 g) nondairy butter (to taste)

Salt and pepper, to taste

☾ THE NIGHT BEFORE:

To make the steak and coating: Heat the olive oil in a skillet over medium heat. Combine the flour, garlic powder, marjoram, basil, celery seed, pepper, and salt in a bowl. If the seitan steaks are not wet from being stored in the cooking broth, dip them into water to wet. Dredge the wet seitan in the dry mixture and coat the steaks. Add to the skillet and brown them a bit on both sides; there is no need to cook through. Remove and store in the fridge.

☼ IN THE MORNING:

To make the cooking broth: Oil the crock of your slow cooker. Combine the water and bouillon. Place the seitan on top, trying to keep at least the bottom of the seitan in the broth. The flour coating will help the liquid thicken up during the cooking process. Loosely place a piece of parchment paper or aluminum foil over the top and place the potatoes on top. Cook on low for 6 to 8 hours.

About 20 minutes before serving, transfer the potatoes to a large bowl. Remove the steaks and transfer to a plate, then add the milk to the gravy and stir to combine. Return the steaks to the slow cooker. Check to see if the broth has thickened into a nice gravy. If the sauce is too thick, add more broth or water. If not, remove the seitan and blend 3 tablespoons (24 g) flour into the gravy. If it is still too thin, add the remaining 2 tablespoons (16 g) flour. Return the seitan to the slow cooker, and turn up to high.

To make the potatoes: Mash the potatoes in a bowl with the milk, butter, salt, and pepper. Keep warm over low heat, covered, while the steaks finish off in the slow cooker.

Place steak over mashed potatoes and top with gravy.

YIELD: 4 servings
TOTAL PREP TIME: 20 minutes
TOTAL COOKING TIME: 6 to 8 hours

CHICK'N NORMANDY WITH APPLES AND BRANDY SAUCE

▶ SOY-FREE

This is another hearty recipe that's perfect for fall. Serve over mashed potatoes or steamed rice with Southern-Style Green Beans (page 142).

INGREDIENTS:

2 tablespoons (30 ml) olive oil

1 small onion, chopped

2 cloves garlic, minced

2 medium-size apples, peeled, cored, and sliced

1¾ cups (410 ml) apple juice or apple cider

¼ cup (60 ml) brandy

1½ tablespoons (9 g) vegan chicken-flavored bouillon or 3 tablespoons (18 g) Chickeny Bouillon (page 19)

1 teaspoon dried basil

1 teaspoon dried thyme

Salt and pepper, to taste

4 to 6 chicken-flavored seitan breasts, store-bought or homemade (page 21)

2 to 3 tablespoons (16 to 24 g) flour

☾ THE NIGHT BEFORE:

Heat the oil in a skillet over medium heat and sauté the onion until translucent, 3 to 5 minutes. Add the garlic and sauté for 2 minutes longer. Store in an airtight container in the fridge.

☀ IN THE MORNING:

Oil the crock of your slow cooker. combine the sautéed onion, apples, apple juice, brandy, bouillon, basil, thyme, and salt and pepper in the slow cooker. Add the chick'n seitan and push down to submerge the chicken in the liquid as much as possible. Cook on low for 6 to 8 hours.

About 30 minutes before serving, remove the chick'n and set aside on a plate. Taste the sauce and adjust the seasonings. Whisk in the flour, return the chick'n to the cooker, and turn up the slow cooker to high. Cook until the sauce is thickened. If you have an older slow cooker you may need to prop up the lid with a wooden spoon to let moisture escape.

YIELD: 4 to 6 servings
TOTAL PREP TIME: 15 minutes
TOTAL COOKING TIME: 6 to 8 hours

CHICK'N MARSALA

▶ SOY-FREE* ▶ GLUTEN-FREE**

This is an earthy-tasting meal that's good enough for company. It does have more prep than most recipes, so if you are in a hurry you might want to pick another dish. Just be sure to come back and try it later! The Marsala wine creates a rich sauce that's flavored with mushrooms and garlic. It's a great date night dinner. Serve over cooked rice or pasta with your favorite steamed veggies and a salad for a complete meal.

INGREDIENTS:

2 tablespoons (30 ml) olive oil

½ onion, minced

2 cloves garlic, minced

8 ounces (225 g) sliced mushrooms

½ cup (60 g) flour, plus 1 tablespoon (8 g) extra, as needed

Salt and pepper, to taste

4 chicken-flavored *seitan breasts, store-bought or homemade (page 21), or thick slices pressed **tofu

1 tablespoon (6 g) vegan chicken-flavored bouillon or 2 tablespoons (12 g) Chickeny Bouillon (page 19)

1 cup (235 ml) water

1 cup (235 ml) Marsala wine

Cooked rice or pasta, for serving

☾ THE NIGHT BEFORE:

Heat the oil in a skillet over medium heat and sauté the onion until translucent, 3 to 5 minutes. Add the garlic and mushrooms and sauté until the mushrooms give off their water and begin to brown, about 10 minutes. Store in an airtight container in the fridge. In a small bowl, combine the ½ cup (60 g) flour, salt, and pepper. If the seitan is not wet, wet it with some water. Then dredge the seitan in the flour mixture, turning to coat. Preheat a nonstick pan over medium heat, add the seitan, and cook on both sides to color slightly, 5 to 10 minutes. Store in an airtight container in the fridge.

☀ IN THE MORNING:

Oil the crock of your slow cooker. Add the sautéed onion, garlic, and mushrooms to the slow cooker. Mix the bouillon into the water and add to the crock with the wine. Layer the seitan on top. It's best if at least the bottom of the seitan pieces are in the broth. The flour coating will help the liquid thicken up during the cooking process. Cook on low for 6 to 8 hours.

About 30 minutes before serving, check to see if the broth has thickened into a nice gravy. If the sauce is too thick, add more broth or water. If it is too thin, remove the seitan to a plate and stir the remaining 1 tablespoon (8 g) flour into the gravy, and return the seitan to the slow cooker. Turn up the slow cooker to high and cook about 30 minutes longer. Taste and adjust the seasonings.

YIELD: 4 servings
TOTAL PREP TIME: 30 minutes
TOTAL COOKING TIME: 6 to 8 hours

CHAPTER 8

SUPER-EASY SIDE DISHES

I love using my slow cooker for side dishes. It's especially handy when you have an elaborate holiday dinner. Not only will it free up the stove for other dishes, but it will also keep food warm until you can get everyone to sit down to eat.

Making side dishes in slow cookers also makes quick work of setting up a buffet. It's a great reason to have more than one slow cooker on hand.

You can cook most veggies in the slow cooker, but make sure you don't overcook delicate ones, such as asparagus, broccoli, and the like. Root vegetables can cook much longer.

1. Sweet Herbed Beets
2. Fruity Rutabagas
3. Fantastic Faux Mashed Potatoes
4. Creamy Scalloped Potatoes
5. Asian Greens
6. Holiday Sweet Potato Casserole

7. Super-Simple Roasted Veggies
8. Creamed Corn with Truffle Oil
9. Balsamic Brussels Sprouts
10. Southern-Style Green Beans
11. Vodka and Dill-Glazed Baby Carrots
12. Slow-Cooked Apple and Sausage Stuffing

SWEET HERBED BEETS

▸ SOY-FREE ▸ GLUTEN-FREE

I love beets and I always have. To me they are sweet, tasty treats.
My other half says they taste like dirt to her, but they just taste nice and
earthy to me. The mint complements the natural sweetness of the beets.

*Note: This recipe uses a 1½- to 2-quart (1.4 to 1.9 L) slow
cooker or a small ovenproof dish in a larger slow cooker.
You can easily double or triple the recipe and use a larger
slow cooker.*

INGREDIENTS:

4 beets

½ cup (120 ml) water

2 sprigs fresh thyme or 2 teaspoons dried

1 teaspoon crushed mint leaves (fresh or dried)

Salt, to taste

☾ THE NIGHT BEFORE:

Peel and dice the beets. Make sure you're not wearing your
favorite clothes, because the beet juice will stain. Store in
an airtight container in the fridge.

☀ IN THE MORNING:

Combine all the ingredients in your small slow cooker.
Cook on low for 6 to 8 hours. Remove and discard the
thyme sprigs and taste and adjust the seasonings.

YIELD: 4 servings
TOTAL PREP TIME: 5 minutes
TOTAL COOKING TIME: 6 to 8 hours

SERVING SUGGESTIONS

You can eat these warm or store them in the fridge to
add to your salads all week long.

FRUITY RUTABAGAS

▸ SOY-FREE ▸ GLUTEN-FREE

Rutabagas aren't the sexiest vegetable around, but maybe you can at least show people how tasty they can be. Rutabagas are sometimes a little bitter, but the sweetness of the pears and apples melt down into a sauce that elevates this side dish to a delectable standout.

INGREDIENTS:

3 medium-size rutabagas, peeled and chopped

1 large onion, thinly sliced

3 large apples, peeled, cored, and chopped

2 pears, peeled, cored, and chopped

1 cup (235 ml) water

Juice of ¼ lemon

Salt and pepper, to taste

☾ **THE NIGHT BEFORE:**

Combine the cut-up vegetables and fruit in an airtight container, add the water and lemon juice, and store in the fridge.

☀ **IN THE MORNING:**

Oil the crock of your slow cooker. Combine all the ingredients in the slow cooker. Cook on low for 6 to 8 hours. Taste and adjust the seasonings.

YIELD: 8 servings
TOTAL PREP TIME: 10 minutes
TOTAL COOKING TIME: 6 to 8 hours

RECIPE IDEAS & VARIATIONS

Can't find rutabagas? This recipe works with turnips, potatoes, carrots, and parsnips too!

FANTASTIC FAUX MASHED POTATOES

▸ GLUTEN-FREE

Sometimes you need something lighter or different from the same old mashed potatoes. Last year I was on an eating plan that cut out potatoes and I had to make a substitute or I wouldn't make it though the winter. These are light and creamy, the perfect mashed potato pretender.

INGREDIENTS:

1 large head cauliflower, broken into small florets (frozen is fine too)

4 medium-size parsnips, peeled if not organic and chopped

½ cup (120 ml) water

2 cloves garlic, minced

½ to 1 cup (120 to 235 ml) unsweetened nondairy milk

¼ cup (56 g) nondairy butter

Salt and pepper, to taste

☾ THE NIGHT BEFORE:

Store the prepared vegetables in an airtight container in the fridge.

☀ IN THE MORNING:

Place the cauliflower, parsnips, and water in the slow cooker. Cook on low for 6 to 8 hours.

Before serving, pour out some of the water, if needed—you don't want this to be too soupy. Add ½ cup (120 ml) of the milk and the butter purée with an immersion blender or in a food processor. You have to keep at it until they look like mashed potatoes. (They will—I promise!) Add the remaining ½ cup (120 ml) milk if they are too stiff. Season to taste with salt and pepper.

YIELD: 4 servings
TOTAL PREP TIME: 10 minutes
TOTAL COOKING TIME: 6 to 8 hours

SERVING SUGGESTION

Use leftovers to make a creamy soup. Just add to steamed veggies, chick'n bouillon, and water and then purée it all together.

CREAMY SCALLOPED POTATOES

▶ SOY-FREE*   ▶ GLUTEN-FREE

Creamy, garlicky potatoes are a favorite anytime, but it's a great dish to bring to a holiday dinner. It's also a great side for Atomic Tofu Pecan Loaf (page 96).

FOR THE SAUCE:

1 cup (135 g) cashews

1 cup (96 g) nutritional yeast

5 cloves garlic

1½ cups (355 ml) unsweetened nondairy milk (*use rice or almond milk)

½ to 1 teaspoon salt (to taste)

Pepper, to taste

2 pounds (910 g) potatoes, peeled (if not organic)

☾ THE NIGHT BEFORE:

To make the sauce: In a food processor or blender combine the sauce ingredients. Blend until smooth and creamy. Store in an airtight container in the fridge.

Thinly slice the potatoes and place in a bowl of cold water (to prevent discoloration). Cover and refrigerate.

☀ IN THE MORNING:

Oil the crock of your slow cooker. Pour one-third of the sauce on the bottom of the crock. Place half of the potatoes on top, then pour on another one-third of the sauce and repeat the layers one more time, ending with the sauce. Cook on low for 6 to 8 hours.

YIELD: 6 servings
TOTAL PREP TIME: 15 minutes
TOTAL COOKING TIME: 6 to 8 hours

RECIPE IDEAS & VARIATIONS

Fancy up this dish and make it au gratin. Just add some shredded vegan cheddar cheese in between the layers of potatoes (but not on top of the casserole). About 30 minutes before serving, sprinkle more cheddar on top of the casserole and cook until melted.

ASIAN GREENS

▶ GLUTEN-FREE*

Greens are the perfect veggie to eat in the winter. Some people can't deal with the bitterness, and the Asian flavors really help mask it. Getting my other half to eat them was a true feat, one that could have only been done with soy sauce and sesame oil. Mix and match different kinds of greens, such as collards, kale, turnip greens, beet greens, and Swiss chard, to find your perfect blend.

....

INGREDIENTS:

1 bunch greens

1 clove garlic, minced

1 teaspoon grated fresh ginger

1 tablespoon (15 ml) soy sauce (*use gluten free)

1 teaspoon rice wine vinegar

1 tablespoon (15 ml) sesame oil or chili sesame oil

☾ THE NIGHT BEFORE:

Wash and cut up the greens. Combine with the garlic and ginger and store in an airtight container in the fridge.

☀ IN THE MORNING:

Oil the crock of your slow cooker. Add the greens, garlic, ginger, soy sauce, and vinegar. Cook on low for 6 to 8 hours. Drizzle each serving with sesame oil, or use chili oil for more of a kick.

YIELD: 6 servings
TOTAL PREP TIME: 10 minutes
TOTAL COOKING TIME: 6 to 8 hours

DID YOU KNOW?

Many kinds of greens, such as collards, actually get sweeter after they go through a frost.

HOLIDAY SWEET POTATO CASSEROLE

▶ GLUTEN-FREE*

Every family seems to have a special recipe for sweet potato casserole. This one is
less sweet than the sticky sweet casserole of my youth. It skips the caramel and marshmallow
that are sometimes included. You could add vegan versions of both if you really want to.
After all, any day is a holiday when you get to eat sweet potato casserole!

FOR THE TOPPING:

2 tablespoons (28 g) nondairy butter

3 tablespoons (45 ml) olive oil

¾ cup (170 g) packed brown sugar

¼ cup (30 g) whole wheat flour
(*use gluten-free baking mix)

3 tablespoons (45 ml) nondairy milk or water

INGREDIENTS:

8 large sweet potatoes, peeled and cut into chunks

½ cup (55 g) chopped pecans

1½ cups (355 ml) water

¼ to ½ teaspoon cinnamon (to taste)

¼ teaspoon grated nutmeg

⅛ teaspoon allspice

Pinch of ground cloves

¼ to ½ cup (60 to 120 ml) plain or vanilla-flavored
nondairy milk

☾ THE NIGHT BEFORE:

To make the topping: Combine all the topping ingredients
in a large bowl and mix thoroughly. Store the topping
and the cut-up sweet potatoes in airtight containers in
the fridge. Store the chopped pecans in a covered bowl,
unrefrigerated.

☼ IN THE MORNING:

Oil the crock of your slow cooker. Add the sweet potatoes
and water. Cook on low for 6 to 8 hours.

About 30 to 45 minutes before serving, turn up the slow
cooker to high. Mash the sweet potatoes in the crock. Add
the cinnamon, nutmeg, allspice, cloves, and ¼ cup (60 ml)
of the nondairy milk and stir to combine. Add the remaining ¼ cup (60 ml) milk if the potatoes are still too stiff,
but leave it out if they are runny. Drop spoonfuls of the
topping onto the sweet potatoes. As the topping begins
to melt, spread it evenly with the back of a spoon. Sprinkle
on the nuts. Serve once the topping is melted and heated
throughout.

YIELD: 8 servings
TOTAL PREP TIME: 15 minutes
TOTAL COOKING TIME: 6 to 8 hours

SUPER-SIMPLE ROASTED VEGGIES

► SOY-FREE ► GLUTEN-FREE

No matter what size slow cooker you have, you can double or halve this recipe to fit it perfectly.

INGREDIENTS:

1 medium-size head cauliflower, broken into florets

16 brussels sprouts

16 baby carrots

16 pearl onions

¼ cup (60 ml) water

2 tablespoons (12 g) vegan chicken-flavored bouillon or 4 tablespoons (24 g) Chickeny Bouillon (page 19)

1 to 2 tablespoons (15 to 30 ml) olive oil

2 sprigs fresh thyme or 2 teaspoons dried

1 sprig fresh rosemary or 1 teaspoon dried

1 teaspoon rubbed sage

Salt and pepper, to taste

DIRECTIONS:

Oil the crock of your slow cooker. Combine all the ingredients in the slow cooker. Cook on low for 4 to 5 hours, or until the veggies are tender. Taste and adjust the seasonings.

YIELD: 6 servings
TOTAL PREP TIME: 15 minutes
TOTAL COOKING TIME: 4 to 5 hours

RECIPE IDEAS & VARIATIONS

This is a perfect side dish anytime of the year, just vary the veggies according to the season. Remember to add any quick-cooking ones, such as spinach, broccoli, or green beans, in the last 30 minutes so they don't overcook.

CREAMED CORN WITH TRUFFLE OIL

▸ SOY-FREE ▸ GLUTEN-FREE

Truffle oil is expensive, but a small bottle will last a long time. You can make this recipe without the truffle oil and it will still taste really good. But the truffle oil takes it to a whole other ethereal level, and smells as wonderful as it tastes. You can always drop hints that you'd like some around your birthday like I do!

Note: This recipe uses a 1½- to 2-quart (1.4 to 1.9 L) slow cooker or a small ovenproof dish in a larger slow cooker. You can double or triple the recipe and use a larger slow cooker if you like.

INGREDIENTS:

1 package (16 ounces, or 454 g) frozen corn kernels

½ cup (120 ml) plain or unsweetened nondairy milk

½ teaspoon salt (or to taste)

Pepper, to taste

1 tablespoon (8 g) cornstarch dissolved in 1 tablespoon (15 ml) warm water

1 tablespoon (15 ml) truffle oil

DIRECTIONS:

Oil the crock of your slow cooker. Combine the corn, milk, salt, and pepper in the slow cooker. Cook on high for 1 to 1½ hours, stirring every 30 minutes, or until the corn is heated through.

Add the cornstarch mixture and truffle oil and stir to combine. It should thicken up quickly. If not, cook for another 10 to 15 minutes.

YIELD: 2 large servings
TOTAL PREP TIME: 5 minutes
TOTAL COOKING TIME: 1 to 1½ hours

RECIPE IDEAS & VARIATIONS

- If you make this without truffle oil, add 1 tablespoon (15 ml) olive oil or (14 g) nondairy butter.

- If you defrost the corn ahead of time or use fresh, the cooking time will be shorter.

BALSAMIC BRUSSELS SPROUTS

▸ SOY-FREE ▸ GLUTEN-FREE

I am a brussels sprouts lover and I'm not ashamed to admit it. This is an easy side dish that you can throw in a 1- to 1½-quart (0.9 to 1.4 L) slow cooker while you are making dinner, or better yet, while you relax before dinner!

Note: This recipe uses a 1- to 1½-quart (0.9 to 1.4 L) slow cooker or a small ovenproof dish in a larger slow cooker.

INGREDIENTS:

8 ounces (225 g) brussels sprouts

1 tablespoon (14 ml) balsamic vinegar

2 tablespoons (30 ml) red wine or an extra 1 tablespoon (15 ml) balsamic

4 sprigs fresh thyme or 1 teaspoon dried

½ teaspoon agave nectar or maple syrup

½ cup (120 ml) water

Salt and pepper, to taste

☽ THE NIGHT BEFORE:

Cut the brussels sprouts into quarters and store in an airtight container in the fridge.

About 2 hours before you want to eat, combine all the ingredients in the slow cooker. Cook on high for 2 hours. Remove and discard the thyme sprigs. Taste and adjust the seasonings.

YIELD: 4 servings
TOTAL PREP TIME: 5 minutes
TOTAL COOKING TIME: 2 hours on high (or 4 hours on low if that fits your schedule better)

SERVING SUGGESTIONS

Try eating the leftovers straight from the fridge, or in a chilled pasta salad.

SOUTHERN-STYLE GREEN BEANS

▶ SOY-FREE ▶ GLUTEN-FREE

In the southern United States they have a thing called a vegetable plate. Vegans, don't let it fool you. Almost all veggies in the South are traditionally cooked with pork fat. There is nothing less vegan-friendly. But these beans are especially for vegans and get their traditional smoked flavor from liquid smoke. You can easily double this recipe for a holiday side dish.

INGREDIENTS:

1 pound (454 g) fresh or frozen green beans, ends cut off

½ cup (120 ml) water

1 teaspoon liquid smoke

½ to 1 teaspoon Cajun seasoning

Salt and pepper, to taste

DIRECTIONS:

Oil the crock of your slow cooker and add all the ingredients. Cook on high for 1½ to 2 hours. Taste and adjust the seasonings.

YIELD: 4 servings
TOTAL PREP TIME: 2 minutes
TOTAL COOKING TIME: 1½ to 2 hours

DID YOU KNOW?

Green beans have vitamins K, C, and A, plus fiber and manganese.

VODKA AND DILL-GLAZED BABY CARROTS

▶ SOY-FREE ▶ GLUTEN-FREE

Sometimes you need a side dish with a little zip. The vodka, bouillon, and dill cook down into a tasty sauce that isn't plain or overpowering. It's just right.

Note: This recipe uses a 1½- to 2-quart (1.4 to 1.9 L) slow cooker or a small ovenproof dish in a larger slow cooker. You can double or triple the recipe and use a larger slow cooker.

INGREDIENTS:

1 pound (454 g) baby carrots

½ cup (120 ml) water

2 tablespoons (30 ml) vodka

2 tablespoons (12 g) vegan chicken-flavored bouillon or 4 tablespoons (24 g) Chickeny Bouillon (page 19)

2 teaspoons dill

Salt and pepper, to taste

DIRECTIONS:

Oil the crock of your slow cooker and add all the ingredients. Cook on low for 6 to 8 hours. Taste and adjust the seasonings.

YIELD: 4 servings
TOTAL PREP TIME: 1 minute
TOTAL COOKING TIME: 6 to 8 hours

A WORTHY NOTE

Carrots are the reigning queen of vitamin A. Just ½ cup (60 g) of cooked carrots provides almost three times the daily recommended amount.

SLOW-COOKED APPLE AND SAUSAGE STUFFING

▶ SOY-FREE*

This is a perfect side dish to bring to an omnivore holiday dinner.
It helps me avoid the hidden meat that could be lurking in other stuffings.

INGREDIENTS:

2 tablespoons (30 ml) olive oil

1 small onion, minced

2 cloves garlic, minced

4 stalks celery, minced

2 apples, peeled, cored, and chopped

1 package (10 ounces, or 280 g) organic stuffing
    or diced stale bread

2 cups (470 ml) water

2 tablespoons (12 g) vegan chicken-flavored bouillon
    or 4 tablespoons (24 g) Chickeny Bouillon (page 19)

½ pound (225 g) sausage crumbles, cooked, or
    *Apple Sage Sausage (page 23)

Salt, to taste

DIRECTIONS:

Heat the oil in a skillet over medium heat and sauté the onion until translucent, 3 to 5 minutes. Add the garlic and celery and sauté for 3 to 4 minutes longer, until the celery is soft. Oil the crock of your slow cooker. Combine the sautéed vegetables with the remaining ingredients in the slow cooker. Cook on high for 2 to 3 hours with the lid propped up on the handle of a wooden spoon, stirring every 20 to 30 minutes.

YIELD: 8 servings
TOTAL PREP TIME: 20 minutes
TOTAL COOKING TIME: 2 to 3 hours

A WORTHY NOTE

Be sure to read the labels on bags of stuffing before buying, because many have chicken in them.

CHAPTER 9

SANDWICH, TORTILLA, AND TACO FILLINGS

It's just one more amazing thing that sandwich, burrito, and taco fillings can all be made in advance in the slow cooker. From the typical Sloppy Joe–style sandwich to the more unusual pesto winter squash, these recipes let you really add some variety to a midweek dinner or weekend lunch.

Don't forget you can fill some of your vegetables, too. By using your slow cooker instead of an oven, you'll have a dish ready to serve as soon as you get home. You can use any leftover grains, beans, or chopped stale bread (think Thanksgiving stuffing) to make fillings for winter squash, summer squash, bell peppers, or cabbage leaves. Think of these recipes as a jumping-off point and see what filling experiments you want to try next.

1. New Orleans Po' Boy
2. Philadelphia-Style Cheesy Portobello Sandwich
3. Tempeh Tornado
4. Texas-Style Tofu Taco Filling
5. Mashed Potato and Edamame Burrito Filling
6. Burst of Flavor Butternut Squash and Pesto Panini Filling
7. Asian Tempeh Lettuce Wraps
8. Acorn Squash Stuffed with Cranberry-Pecan Rice
9. Chick'n Verde

NEW ORLEANS PO' BOY

Po' boys are a staple in New Orleans cuisine, but if you want a vegan one it's time to make your own. This recipe recreates that messy po' boy experience.

INGREDIENTS:

3 cups (330 g) cubed beef-flavored seitan, store-bought or homemade (page 22)

2 cloves garlic, minced

2 cups (470 ml) water or broth from homemade seitan, plus more as needed

2 tablespoons (12 g) vegan beef-flavored bouillon or 4 tablespoons (24 g) Beefy Bouillon (page 20)

½ teaspoon Cajun seasoning (optional)

Salt and pepper, to taste

2 to 4 tablespoons (16 to 32 g) flour or 1 to 1½ tablespoons (8 to 12 g) cornstarch, as needed

French bread, for serving

☾ THE NIGHT BEFORE:

Thinly slice half of the seitan. Grate or pulse the remaining half in a food processor until you have small ragged bits. Store in an airtight container in the fridge.

☼ IN THE MORNING:

Combine the seitan, garlic, water, bouillon, Cajun seasoning, and salt and pepper in the slow cooker. Cook on low for 6 to 8 hours.

About 20 minutes before serving, add extra water if the mixture has become dry. Add 2 tablespoons (16 g) flour or 1 tablespoon (8 g) cornstarch to the slow cooker and mix well. Cook for 20 more minutes. This should thicken the gravy. If it is not thick enough, add the remaining 2 tablespoons (16 g) flour or ½ tablespoon (4 g) cornstarch. Serve on French bread.

YIELD: 4 servings
TOTAL PREP TIME: 15 minutes
TOTAL COOKING TIME: 6 to 8 hours

SERVING SUGGESTION

Serve it on a soft French baguette. Add vegan mayo, lettuce, and tomato to make it "dressed."

PHILADELPHIA-STYLE CHEESY PORTOBELLO SANDWICH

This is a quick and easy sandwich filling that's ready when you get home. Add a salad or some pasta salad and you have a causal dinner for friends with almost no work.

....

INGREDIENTS:

1 medium-size onion, cut into strips

2 large bell peppers, cut into strips

4 large portobello mushrooms, sliced

2 tablespoons (12 g) vegan beef- or chicken-flavored bouillon or 4 tablespoons (24 g) Beefy Bouillon (page 20) or Chickeny Bouillon (page 19)

½ cup (120 ml) water

Salt and pepper, to taste

1 tablespoon (8 g) cornstarch

6 whole wheat hoagie rolls, toasted, for serving

Shredded vegan cheddar cheese, for serving

☾ THE NIGHT BEFORE:

Store the sliced onion, peppers, and mushrooms in an airtight container in the fridge.

☀ IN THE MORNING:

Oil the crock of your slow cooker. Mix the bouillon with the water and pour into the slow cooker. Add the onion, bell peppers, mushrooms, and salt and pepper. Cook on low for 6 to 8 hours.

About 20 minutes before serving, stir the cornstarch into the gravy and mix well. Cook for 20 more minutes. This should thicken the gravy. Taste and adjust the seasonings.

Spoon some of the hot sandwich mixture onto each toasted bun and top with the cheddar.

YIELD: 6 servings
TOTAL PREP TIME: 10 minutes
TOTAL COOKING TIME: 6 to 8 hours

TEMPEH TORNADO

▶ GLUTEN-FREE*

Okay, so this is really just a Sloppy Joe, Manwich, or whatever they call a hearty meat sauce sandwich in your part of the world. It's easy to throw together in the morning before work and can easily cook all day. If you will be gone more than 9 hours, add a little more water. You can make half of the recipe in a 1½- or 2-quart (1.4 or 1.9 L) slow cooker if you don't want to make this much.

....

INGREDIENTS:

2 packages (8 ounces, or 225 g each) tempeh
  (*use plain soy tempeh), cubed

3 cloves garlic

½ bell pepper

4 or 12 buns, for serving

FOR THE SAUCE:

1 can (28 ounces, or 784 g) diced tomatoes or 3 cups
  (540 g) chopped fresh

½ cup (120 ml) water

1 tablespoon (6 g) vegan chicken-flavored bouillon
  or 2 tablespoons (12 g) Chickeny Bouillon (page 19)

1 tablespoon (16 g) tomato paste

1 tablespoon (15 ml) agave nectar or maple syrup

1 tablespoon (15 ml) apple cider, plain white, or
  wine vinegar

1 teaspoon molasses

1 teaspoon vegan Worcestershire sauce

½ teaspoon liquid smoke

½ teaspoon cumin

½ teaspoon chipotle chile powder or smoked paprika

½ teaspoon pasilla chile or regular chili powder

½ teaspoon salt

¼ to ½ teaspoon hot pepper sauce (to taste)

☾ THE NIGHT BEFORE:

Steam the tempeh in a steamer basket for 10 minutes. This takes out some of the bitterness. While the tempeh is cooking, mince the garlic and bell pepper.

To make the sauce: Place all the sauce ingredients in a large bowl and stir to combine. Add the tempeh, garlic, and pepper, cover, and store in the fridge.

☀ IN THE MORNING:

Add all the ingredients to the slow cooker. Cook on low for 6 to 8 hours. Taste and adjust the seasonings. For open-faced sandwiches, split 4 buns and top each of the 8 slices with one-eighth of the mixture. For regular sanwiches, split 12 buns, top each bottom half with a smaller dollop of the mixture, and replace the top half.

YIELD: 12 regular sandwiches or 8 open-faced sandwiches
TOTAL PREP TIME: 15 minutes
TOTAL COOKING TIME: 6 to 8 hours

TEXAS-STYLE TOFU TACO FILLING

▶ GLUTEN-FREE*

Tex-Mex food is simple, nutritious, and filling. These tacos are easy to throw together, and you can use the filling for burritos, nachos, or any of your favorites. Depending on how much liquid is left, you may want to serve with a slotted spoon so you don't disintegrate your taco.

....

Note: This recipe uses a 1½- to 2-quart (1.4 to 1.9 L) slow cooker or a small ovenproof dish in a larger slow cooker. You can double or triple the recipe and use a larger one if you like.

INGREDIENTS:

1 package (15 ounces, or 425 g) firm tofu, cubed

1 clove garlic, minced

Zest and juice of 1 lime

3 tablespoons (50 g) salsa

½ teaspoon chili powder

¼ teaspoon chipotle chile powder or smoked paprika

¼ teaspoon cumin

Hot pepper, to taste

Salt, to taste

6 hard corn tortilla taco shells, warmed, for serving (*use gluten-free)

☾ THE NIGHT BEFORE:

Combine the cubed tofu, minced garlic, and zest and lime juice in an airtight container in the fridge.

☀ IN THE MORNING:

Oil the crock of your slow cooker. Add all the ingredients and cook on low for 6 to 8 hours. Taste and adjust the seasonings. Serve in warmed corn tortilla shells.

YIELD: 6 servings
TOTAL PREP TIME: 15 minutes
TOTAL COOKING TIME: 6 to 8 hours

SERVING SUGGESTION

Serve this with Mashed Potato Edamame Burritos (page 151) and Spanish Quinoa (page 107).

MASHED POTATO AND EDAMAME BURRITO FILLING

▸ GLUTEN-FREE*

From the first time I had a potato burrito, I was hooked!
I've healthied it up a bit with a few veggies and some edamame.

INGREDIENTS:

4 large russet potatoes, peeled if not organic and cut into chunks

1 cup (235 ml) water

1½ cups (390 ml) mild salsa

1 pound (454 g) mix of corn, chopped red bell pepper, and edamame (I use a frozen mix from Trader Joe's)

Salt, to taste

6 to 8 tortillas, for serving (*use gluten-free)

☾ THE NIGHT BEFORE:

Store the prepared potatoes in an airtight container in the fridge.

☀ IN THE MORNING:

Oil the crock of your slow cooker. Add the potatoes, water, and salsa and cook on low for 6 to 8 hours.

About 1 hour before serving, mash the potatoes with a potato masher or an immersion blender. Add the mixed vegetables and salt and cook until heated through. Taste and adjust the seasonings. Serve the filling wrapped in tortillas.

YIELD: 6 to 8 servings
TOTAL PREP TIME: 5 minutes
TOTAL COOKING TIME: 6 to 8 hours

A WORTHY NOTE

If you get low-fat tortillas it helps to steam them before rolling the filling in them. I just put them on top of the filling while it's in the slow cooker for a few seconds to soften.

BURST OF FLAVOR BUTTERNUT SQUASH AND PESTO PANINI FILLING

▶ SOY-FREE ▶ GLUTEN-FREE*

This was inspired by a butternut squash panini that was made for the Bull City Vegan Challenge. Toast is the restaurant that made the original sandwich. Be sure to visit them if you are ever in Durham, North Carolina.

INGREDIENTS:

1 medium-size butternut squash

3 or 4 fresh sage leaves

4 fresh rosemary leaves

Leaves from 1 thyme sprig

$\frac{1}{2}$ cup (60 g) walnuts

2 tablespoons (15 ml) olive oil

$\frac{1}{4}$ cup (48 g) nutritional yeast

12 slices bread, for serving (*use gluten-free)

☾ THE NIGHT BEFORE:

Get a whole butternut squash that will fit into your slow cooker. Poke holes in it and cook it in the slow cooker on low overnight, 6 to 8 hours. (No water or oil is needed.)

☼ IN THE MORNING:

Remove the squash from the slow cooker and let cool for about 30 minutes, then store in the fridge.

When ready to serve, remove the squash from the fridge and cut it in half. Scrape out the seeds. Scoop out $1\frac{1}{2}$ to 2 cups (385 to 510 g) of the flesh to use for this recipe, and store or freeze the rest for another dish or to remake this one at a later date.

Make the pesto by combining the herbs, walnuts, and olive oil in a food processor and pulse until it's grainy but not puréed. Mix the pesto and the nutritional yeast into the soft squash. Spread on 6 slices of bread, top each with the remaining 6 slices of bread and cook on the stove top. Use a panini pan if you have one. As an alternative, you can use a pan and a heavy skillet that will fit inside it to press the sandwich, or you could use a grill and a heavy object of your choice.

YIELD: 6 servings
TOTAL PREP TIME: 20 minutes
TOTAL COOKING TIME: 6 to 8 hours

ASIAN TEMPEH LETTUCE WRAPS

▶ GLUTEN-FREE*

In this case, iceberg lettuce can be your friend. I love the crunch you get from biting into it, and its mild flavor really lets the Asian filling stand out. This is the perfect food to make for a light summer dinner because the slow cooker doesn't heat up your house. You can have it ready and waiting for an after-work cocktail party on the deck.

INGREDIENTS:

1 package (8 ounces, or 225 g) tempeh (*use plain soy tempeh), cubed

1 large stalk celery

2 medium-size carrots

1 can (8 ounces, or 225 g) water chestnuts, drained

FOR THE SAUCE:

2 cloves garlic, minced

1 tablespoon (8 g) grated ginger, plus more as needed

1½ cups (355 ml) water

¼ cup (60 ml) soy sauce (*use gluten-free)

¼ cup (60 ml) seasoned rice vinegar or plain rice vinegar mixed with 1 teaspoon sugar

¼ teaspoon red pepper flakes or sriracha

Whole iceberg or butter lettuce leaves, for serving

☾ THE NIGHT BEFORE:

Steam the tempeh in a steamer basket for 10 minutes. This takes out some of the bitterness. While the tempeh is cooking, mince the celery, carrots, and water chestnuts.

To make the sauce: Combine all the sauce ingredients in a large bowl. Add the tempeh, celery, carrots, and water chestnuts, cover, and store in the fridge.

☀ IN THE MORNING:

Place the tempeh, vegetables, and sauce in the slow cooker and smash the tempeh with a spoon until it crumbles. Cook on low for 6 to 8 hours. Taste and adjust the seasonings. Add an additional 1 teaspoon grated ginger if its flavor has dulled. Serve with whole lettuce leaves to wrap the filling in.

YIELD: 6 servings
TOTAL PREP TIME: 15 minutes
TOTAL COOKING TIME: 6 to 8 hours

SERVING SUGGESTION

Use the filling to make a banh mi sandwich. Serve on a toasted sub roll with fresh bean sprouts, shredded carrots, cilantro, and some jalapeños.

ACORN SQUASH STUFFED WITH CRANBERRY-PECAN RICE

▶ SOY-FREE ▶ GLUTEN-FREE

By using your slow cooker instead of an oven, you'll have a dish ready to serve as soon as you get home. Use the recipe below as a jumping-off point. You can use any leftover grains, beans, or chopped stale bread (think Thanksgiving stuffing) to make a filling. Because the acorn squash is a little sweet, I like to add some dried fruit, as well as savory herbs. It's a perfect place to use up that last bit of veggie sausage (cook it first), crumbled baked tofu, or other meat substitute.

....

INGREDIENTS:

1 medium-size acorn squash

Olive oil, for rubbing

1 cup (165 g) cooked brown rice or other precooked grain

1 can (15 ounces, or 420 g) lentils, white beans, or kidney beans, drained and rinsed, or 1½ cups (340 g) homemade (page 17)

1 tablespoon (8 g) chopped dried cranberries

1 tablespoon (7 g) chopped pecans

1 clove garlic, minced

2 sprigs fresh thyme, minced

1 teaspoon chopped fresh rosemary

Salt and pepper, to taste

Water or broth, as needed

☾ THE NIGHT BEFORE:

Cut the acorn squash in half and remove the seeds. Lightly rub the exposed flesh with a little olive oil. Store in an airtight container in the fridge. In a bowl, combine the rice, lentils, cranberries, pecans, garlic, thyme, rosemary, and salt and pepper, stir to mix. Add some water or broth if the mixture is too dry. Cover, and store in the fridge.

☀ IN THE MORNING:

Pour about ½ inch (1.3 cm) water in the bottom of your slow cooker. Crumple up some aluminum foil and place under the squash halves to keep them from turning over and spilling out the stuffing. No aluminum foil? Cut a little off the bottom side of the squash half to get it to sit straight. Fill the squash with the stuffing and round it over the flesh, if possible. Cook on low for 6 to 8 hours, or until the squash is tender when pierced with a fork.

YIELD: 2 servings
TOTAL PREP TIME: 15 minutes
TOTAL COOKING TIME: 6 to 8 hours

A WORTHY NOTE

If you have a large, oval slow cooker you can double this recipe and make 4 servings instead of 2.

CHICK'N VERDE

▶ SOY-FREE

This healthy seitan and green sauce recipe makes a large amount, so it's perfect for a light dinner party with margaritas. It freezes well, too, so make a batch now and enjoy again in a month or two. Tomatillos can be expensive at some stores, but try and find a Latino market near you. They can be as much as one-quarter the price as at a health food store.

FOR THE SAUCE:

1⅔ pounds (755 g) tomatillos, husks removed and cut into chunks

3 cloves garlic, minced

1 can (4 ounces, or 113 g) green chiles

½ cup (120 ml) water

¼ cup (60 ml) apple cider vinegar

3 tablespoons (3 g) chopped fresh cilantro

2 teaspoons mild or hot chili powder

½ to 1 teaspoon salt

Juice of 1 lime

INGREDIENTS:

3 to 4 cups (675 to 900 g) cubed chicken-flavored seitan, store-bought or homemade (page 21)

Steamed rice, 10 tortillas or wraps, or 10 sub rolls, for serving

☾ THE NIGHT BEFORE:

To make the sauce: Add all the sauce ingredients to a blender or food processor and process until smooth. Add the seitan cubes and store in an airtight container in the fridge.

☀ IN THE MORNING:

Oil the crock of your slow cooker. Add the seitan and sauce and cook on low for 6 to 8 hours. Serve over rice, as a burrito filling, or on a sub roll.

YIELD: 10 servings
TOTAL PREP TIME: 15 minutes
TOTAL COOKING TIME: 6 to 8 hours

RECIPE IDEAS & VARIATIONS

Roll leftovers up in tortillas or wraps with rice and freeze for grab-and-go lunches throughout the month.

CHAPTER 10

BEAUTIFUL BREADS *NOT* FROM YOUR OVEN

No one would think a pizza or quick bread could come out of a slow cooker. But basically, a slow cooker is like a small oven, the main difference being the amount of moisture that's present during cooking. The nice thing is that it doesn't heat up the kitchen like an oven, so it's perfect for summer. Plus, it gives you more oven space when you need it for a party.

Keep the moisture from ruining the breads by putting a clean dish towel under the lid to soak up the condensation. You can also place a wooden spoon between the slow cooker and the lid, which will create a space for the condensation to evaporate. The larger the gap, the more it will add to the cooking time, so pick your spoon accordingly.

You can also bake in a loaf pan in your slow cooker. I like the glass ones with no handles. When you are using a pan inside your slow cooker, keep the bottom of the pan slightly elevated from the bottom of the crock. I do this by taking a piece of aluminum foil, rolling it into a rope, and joining the ends into an oval or circle. Then I just place the foil ring in the bottom of the crock and place the pan on top of it. You may need to press just a little to flatten out the foil so your baked goods will be even.

Just like an oven, your slow cooker may have hot spots. I rotate my crock about every hour when I'm baking so one side doesn't cook faster than the other.

1. Chock-full of Veggies Cornbread
2. Scrumptious Strawberry Cornbread
3. Foolproof Focaccia
4. Perfect Pizza From Your Slow Cooker
5. Savory Cheddar Sausage Bread
6. Whole-Wheat Pumpkin Gingerbread
7. Citrusy Rosemary Breakfast Bread
8. Wholesome Chocolate Chip Banana Bread

CHOCK-FULL OF VEGGIES CORNBREAD

▸ SOY-FREE ▸ GLUTEN-FREE

This is a traditional Southern cornbread. It doesn't have any wheat flour in it,
only cornmeal. The moisture of the zucchini replaces the oil to make it easy
on your waistline, too. Cooking it in the slow cooker will make it extra moist.
I like to serve thick and hearty, home-style beans over this for a complete meal.

INGREDIENTS:

1 tablespoon (15 ml) apple cider vinegar

1½ cups (355 ml) nondairy milk

1 tablespoon (7 g) ground flaxseed

3 tablespoons (45 ml) warm water

2 cups (275 g) cornmeal

½ teaspoon salt

1½ teaspoons baking powder

½ teaspoon baking soda

1 cup (132 g) fresh or frozen corn kernels

½ cup (75 g) chopped bell pepper

½ cup (60 g) shredded zucchini

DIRECTIONS:

Add the vinegar to the milk and set aside for 5 minutes.
Mix the flaxseed with the warm water to make a paste. In
a large bowl, combine the cornmeal, salt, baking powder,
and baking soda. Add the milk mixture, flaxseed mixture,
corn, pepper, and zucchini to the bowl. Mix until combined. If your zucchini is not providing enough moisture to
combine the mixture, add 1 tablespoon (15 ml) water and
mix again.

Pour the mixture into an oiled crock or into an oiled loaf
pan that fits in your slow cooker. Cook on high for 2½
to 3½ hours if cooking in the crock or 3½ to 4½ hours
if cooking in the pan, propping up the lid with a wooden
spoon to all the condensation to escape. After 2 hours,
stick a fork in the center and see if it comes out clean;
if not, cook longer and check again. The center will still
stay moister than it would if it were oven baked, but you
will see a difference on the fork as it continues to cook.
Remember, if you cook it in a loaf pan, it will continue to
cook a little more after you remove it from the slow cooker.

YIELD: 1 loaf
TOTAL PREP TIME: 15 minutes
TOTAL COOKING TIME: 2½ to 3½ hours if cooked in the
crock, 3½ to 4½ hours if cooked in the pan

SERVING SUGGESTIONS

• Mix some fresh minced basil or cilantro into some
softened nondairy butter and serve on the side.

• Make leftovers feel new by serving them on top of
lightly toasted leftover cornbread. White Bean and
Kale Stew (page 69) is a perfect pairing.

SCRUMPTIOUS STRAWBERRY CORNBREAD

▸ SOY-FREE ▸ GLUTEN-FREE*

This sweet cornbread is great for breakfast. Like most baked goods cooked in the slow cooker, it is very dense and moist. You can substitute blueberries, or any seasonal berry, if you'd like.

INGREDIENTS:

1 tablespoon (7 g) ground flaxseed

3 tablespoons (45 ml) warm water

1 cup (140 g) cornmeal

1 cup (132 g) whole wheat pastry flour
(*use gluten-free baking mix)

1½ teaspoons baking powder

½ teaspoon baking soda

½ teaspoon salt

6 ounces (170 g) nondairy yogurt (I used coconut)

3 to 5 tablespoons (45 to 75 ml) maple syrup or agave nectar (to taste)

3 tablespoons (45 ml) olive oil

12 ounces (340 g) fresh or frozen strawberries, chopped

SERVING SUGGESTION

Mix some agave nectar into some softened nondairy butter and serve on the side. Add some minced fresh basil for a summery twist.

DIRECTIONS:

Mix the flaxseed with the warm water to make a paste. In a large bowl, combine the cornmeal, flour, baking powder, baking soda, and salt. In a separate bowl, combine the nondairy yogurt, flaxseed mixture, maple syrup, olive oil, and strawberries. Add the wet mixture to the dry and stir to combine. If your strawberries don't provide enough moisture to combine the mixture, add 1 tablespoon (15 ml) water and mix again.

Pour the mixture into an oiled crock or into an oiled loaf pan that fits in your slow cooker. Cook on high for 2½ to 3½ hours if cooking in the crock or 3½ to 4½ hours if cooking in the loaf pan, propping up the lid with a wooden spoon to allow the condensation to escape. After 2 hours, stick a fork in the center and see if it comes out clean; if not, cook longer and check again. The center will still stay moister than it would if it were oven baked, but you will see a difference on the fork as it continues to cook. Remember, if you cook it in a loaf pan, it will continue to cook a little more after you remove it from the slow cooker.

YIELD: 1 loaf
TOTAL PREP TIME: 15 minutes
TOTAL COOKING TIME: 2½ to 3½ hours if cooked in the crock, 3½ to 4½ hours if cooked in the loaf pan

FOOLPROOF FOCACCIA

▶ SOY-FREE

Bread and pizza aren't the first things most people think of when they think of using a slow cooker, but it's perfect for hot summer months, plus you can run errands while the dough is rising or the bread is cooking. This focaccia recipe is easy because it requires no kneading and the dough lasts for 7 days. I make my dough over the weekend and slow cook it throughout the week as I need it.

....

INGREDIENTS:

1 tablespoon (12 g) or 1 packet dry yeast

1½ cups (355 ml) warm water (105° to 115°F [40.5° to 46°C])

½ teaspoon agave nectar or maple syrup

2 tablespoons (30 ml) olive oil, plus more for drizzling

2 cups (240 g) whole wheat flour

1 cup (120 g) white whole wheat or unbleached white flour

1¼ teaspoons salt

Coarse salt, for sprinkling (optional)

Dried or fresh rosemary, for sprinkling (optional)

SERVING SUGGESTION

Top with All-Occasion Roasted Garlic (page 27), Balsamic Onion Marmalade (page 30), or your favorite chopped fresh herbs.

DIRECTIONS:

Combine the yeast, warm water, and agave nectar in a large bowl. Let it sit for 5 to 10 minutes. You should be able to see the difference in the mixture as the yeast grows. The yeast expands and looks almost foamy. When this happens, add the olive oil, flours, and salt and stir with a wooden spoon until combined, or use a mixer with a dough hook. The batter will be very sticky.

Turn the dough out onto a floured cutting board and separate the dough depending on what you plan on making. This recipe makes one thick focaccia, but you can split it in half to make two thinner ones. (You can also make 4 pizzas from this recipe; see page 162.) Store any extra dough in a covered bowl in the fridge for later in the week.

Oil the crock of your slow cooker. Shape the dough to fit the shape of the slow cooker. I like to use a 5½-quart (5 L) oval slow cooker for this, but a round one will work, too. The size and shape of the slow cooker will affect the overall thickness.

Place the shaped dough into the slow cooker. For focaccia, make indentions with your fingers or a fork, drizzle with more olive oil, and sprinkle with coarse salt and chopped rosemary. Let it rise for about 1 hour with the lid on and the slow cooker turned off.

Place a clean dish towel under the lid while it's cooking to absorb the condensation that will otherwise drip down onto your bread and increase the cooking time. Cook on high for 1½ to 2 hours, or until the middle feels springy.

YIELD: Dough for 2 focaccias or 4 pizzas
TOTAL PREP TIME: 20 minutes
TOTAL COOKING TIME: 1 hour to rise, then 1½ to 2 hours to cook

PERFECT PIZZA FROM YOUR SLOW COOKER

It's really surprising just how much you can do in the slow cooker. Pizza is great in the slow cooker on those blistering hot summer days, when you can't bear to turn on the oven. It's also a great treat when you go camping. I bring premade dough, prechopped veggies, and vegan mozzarella in the cooler. You'll be greeted with lots of oohs and aahs by your camping buddies.

This is a free-form recipe. Use as little or as much sauce as you would typically put on your pizza. The same goes for toppings. If you use fresh onion and bell pepper, cut into a small dice and add them at the beginning so they will be cooked by the end.

INGREDIENTS:

¼ recipe Foolproof Focaccia dough (page 161)

¼ to ½ cup (63 to 125 g) tomato sauce

Chopped veggies of choice, such as onion, green pepper, All-Occasion Roasted Garlic (page 27), Balsamic Onion Marmalade (page 30)

½ to 1 cup (62 to 115 g) shredded vegan mozzarella cheese

DIRECTIONS:

Oil the crock of your slow cooker. Shape the dough to fit in the slow cooker. Top with the tomato sauce and then the veggies. Cook on high for 1½ to 2 hours in a large oval slow cooker, or up to 3½ hours in a round 4-quart (3.8 L) slow cooker, propping up the lid with a wooden spoon to allow the condensation to escape.

About 15 minutes before serving, sprinkle with the shredded vegan mozzarella. Serve once the cheese is melted (if you are using a vegan cheese that melts, of course).

YIELD: 4 servings
TOTAL PREP TIME: 15 minutes
TOTAL COOKING TIME: 1½ to 3½ hours

A WORTHY NOTE

This recipe works best in a larger oval slow cooker because the dough will be thinner and cook faster. In a 4-quart (3.8 L) round one it will be more of a thick-crust pizza and will have a longer cooking time.

SAVORY CHEDDAR SAUSAGE BREAD

This is a savory quick bread that has a nice herb flavor
that's complemented by the bite of vegan cheddar cheese.

INGREDIENTS:

2 cups (240 g) whole wheat pastry flour

1 tablespoon (8 g) baking powder

½ teaspoon baking soda

¼ teaspoon salt

Pepper, to taste

2 tablespoons (14 g) ground flaxseed mixed with
    2 tablespoons (30 ml) water

2 tablespoons (30 ml) olive oil

1 cup (235 ml) unsweetened or plain nondairy milk

1½ cups (153 g) sausage crumbles, cooked, or
    Apple Sage Sausage (page 23)

1 cup (115 g) shredded vegan cheddar cheese

DIRECTIONS:

Combine the flour, baking powder, baking soda, salt, and
pepper in a large bowl. In another bowl, combine the flaxseed mixture, oil, and milk. Add the dry mixture to the wet
and stir with a wooden spoon until it is just combined. Stir
in the sausage and cheese.

Pour the mixture into an oiled crock or into an oiled loaf
pan that fits in your slow cooker. Cook on high, propping
up the lid with a wooden spoon to allow the condensation
to escape, for 1½ to 2½ hours if cooked in the crock or 3 to
3½ hours if cooked in the loaf pan, or until the middle feels
springy when touched. Remember, if you cook it in a loaf
pan, it will continue to cook a little more after you remove
it from the slow cooker.

YIELD: 1 loaf
TOTAL PREP TIME: 15 minutes
TOTAL COOKING TIME: 1½ to 2½ hours if cooked in the
crock, 3 to 3½ hours if cooked in the loaf pan

SERVING SUGGESTION

This bread goes great with soups, stews, and salads.
It's also a great on-the-run breakfast. Leftovers are
delicious lightly toasted.

WHOLE-WHEAT PUMPKIN GINGERBREAD

▶ SOY-FREE

This gingerbread gets a nutrition boost and fall flavor from the addition of pumpkin.
You can use canned organic pumpkin, or make your own purée (page 34). The slow
cooker is perfect for gingerbread because things stay moister. You can use regular flour
or even a gluten-free baking mix if you don't have whole wheat pastry flour on hand.

INGREDIENTS:

2 cups (240 g) whole wheat pastry flour

1 tablespoon (8 g) baking powder

½ teaspoon baking soda

1½ tablespoons (8 g) ground ginger

1 teaspoon cinnamon

½ teaspoon ground cloves

½ teaspoon allspice

¼ teaspoon nutmeg

¼ teaspoon salt

2 tablespoons (14 g) ground flaxseed mixed with
2 tablespoons (30 ml) water

1 cup (245 g) pumpkin purée, store-bought or
homemade (page 34)

½ cup (170 g) molasses

½ cup (170 g) agave nectar or maple syrup

¼ cup (60 ml) olive oil

1 teaspoon vanilla extract

DIRECTIONS:

In a large bowl, combine the flour, baking powder, baking
soda, ginger, cinnamon, cloves, allspice, nutmeg, and salt.
In another bowl, combine the flaxseed mixture, pumpkin,
molasses, agave, oil, and vanilla. Add the dry mixture to
the wet and stir with a wooden spoon until just combined.

Pour the mixture into an oiled crock or into an oiled loaf
pan that fits in your slow cooker. Cook on high, propping up
the lid with a wooden spoon to allow the condensation to
escape, for 1½ to 2½ hours if cooked in the crock or 2½ to
3½ hours if cooked in the loaf pan, or until a knife inserted
into the center comes out almost clean. Remember, if you
cook it in a loaf pan, it will continue to cook a little more
after you remove it from the slow cooker.

YIELD: 1 loaf
TOTAL PREP TIME: 15 minutes
TOTAL COOKING TIME: 1½ to 2½ hours if cooked in the
crock, 2½ to 3½ hours if cooked in the loaf pan

RECIPE IDEAS & VARIATIONS

For some extra zing, add 1 teaspoon grated fresh
ginger to the wet ingredients.

CITRUSY ROSEMARY BREAKFAST BREAD

▶ SOY-FREE   ▶ GLUTEN-FREE*

Start the morning with an orangey treat that has a touch of pine from the rosemary. It's made with whole wheat pastry flour, so it's healthier than your average quick bread. This recipe uses sugar, but you can substitute agave nectar or maple syrup if you prefer. You'll just need to add a few more tablespoons of flour to make up for the extra moisture.

INGREDIENTS:

½ cup (100 g) sugar

2 cups (240 g) whole wheat pastry flour (*use gluten-free baking mix)

1 tablespoon (8 g) baking powder

½ teaspoon baking soda

1 tablespoon (2 g) minced fresh rosemary

2 tablespoons (14 g) ground flaxseed mixed with 2 tablespoons (30 ml) water

½ cup (120 g) applesauce

2 tablespoons (30 ml) olive oil

½ cup (120 ml) orange juice

Juice of ½ lemon

1 teaspoon vanilla extract

1 teaspoon orange or lemon extract

DIRECTIONS:

Combine the sugar, flour, baking powder, baking soda, and rosemary in a large bowl. In another bowl, combine the flaxseed mixture, applesauce, oil, orange juice, lemon juice, and extracts. Add the wet mixture to the dry and stir with wooden spoon until just combined.

Pour the mixture into an oiled crock or into an oiled loaf pan that fits in your slow cooker. Cook on high, propping up the lid with a wooden spoon to allow the condensation to escape, for 1½ to 2½ hours if cooked in the crock or 2½ to 3½ hours if cooked in the loaf pan, or until a knife inserted into the center comes out almost clean. Remember, if you cook it in a loaf pan, it will continue to cook a little more after you remove it from the slow cooker.

YIELD: 1 loaf
TOTAL PREP TIME: 15 minutes
TOTAL COOKING TIME: 1½ to 2½ hours if cooked in the crock, 2½ to 3½ hours if cooked in the pan

RECIPE IDEAS & VARIATIONS

Make half the recipe and put into silicon muffin cups. In a 5½- to 6-quart (5.2 to 5.7 L) oval slow cooker, you can fit 6 muffins. The cooking time will shorten to 1 to 1½ hours.

WHOLESOME CHOCOLATE CHIP BANANA BREAD

This traditional sweet banana bread is full of chocolaty goodness
and great for a decadent breakfast or an easy dessert.

INGREDIENTS:

2 cups (240 g) whole wheat pastry flour

1 tablespoon (8 g) baking powder

½ teaspoon baking soda

2 tablespoons (14 g) ground flaxseed mixed with
2 tablespoons (30 ml) water

½ cup (120 g) applesauce

½ cup (100 g) sugar

2 tablespoons (30 ml) olive oil

1 teaspoon vanilla extract

3 bananas, mashed

1 cup (175 g) chocolate chips (I like to use mini chips)

DIRECTIONS:

In a large bowl, combine the flour, baking powder, and baking soda. In another bowl, combine the flaxseed mixture,
applesauce, sugar, oil, vanilla, and bananas. Add the dry
mixture to the wet and stir with a wooden spoon until just
combined. Stir in the chocolate chips.

Pour the mixture into an oiled crock or into an oiled loaf
pan that fits in your slow cooker. Cook on high, propping
up the lid with a wooden spoon to allow the condensation
to escape, for 1½ to 2½ hours if cooked in the crock or
2½ to 3½ hours if cooked in the loaf pan, or until the center feels springy when touched. Remember, if you cook it
in a loaf pan, it will continue to cook a little more after you
remove it from the slow cooker.

YIELD: 1 loaf
TOTAL PREP TIME: 15 minutes
TOTAL COOKING TIME: 1½ to 2½ hours if cooked in the
crock, 2½ to 3½ hours if cooked in the loaf pan

RECIPE IDEAS & VARIATIONS

You can leave out the chocolate chips and add in
the same amount of chopped nuts. Or you can
have your nuts and your chocolate chips too by
using ½ cup (60 g) of each instead.

CHAPTER 11

PARTY SNACKS THAT COOK WHILE YOU'RE GETTING READY

I love throwing parties. At any party you need to have a few nibbles to serve with drinks while all your guests arrive, especially if your friends are like mine and arrive fashionably late. It's part of being a good host, and it keeps everyone's blood sugar at an acceptable level. Most of these recipes use a 1½- to 2-quart (1.4 to 1.9 L) slow cooker. You can double or triple the recipes and use a larger slow cooker, but I didn't think you'd really want 4 quarts (3.8 L) of bean dip (even if you can use the leftovers for burrito filling).

1. Blueberry-Balsamic Meatball Sauce with Rosemary
2. Old-Fashioned Cereal Snack Mix
3. Sweet and Spicy Nut Mix
4. Pimento Cheese Fondue
5. Subtly Spiced Peanut Coconut Fondue
6. Spinach Artichoke Dip
7. Cheesy Chorizo Dip
8. Smoky Bean Dip

BLUEBERRY-BALSAMIC MEATBALL SAUCE WITH ROSEMARY

The inspiration for this recipe comes from theNoshery.com's blog. This savory sauce has sweet flavors of blueberries and raspberries that are balanced out with rosemary and tangy balsamic. Serve over baked vegan meatballs. (I tried making the meatballs in a larger slow cooker with the sauce, but the meatballs completely lost their shape, so I would not recommend doing it that way.)

Note: This recipe uses a 1½- to 2-quart (1.4 to 1.9 L) slow cooker.

INGREDIENTS:

12 ounces (340 g) fresh or frozen blueberries

2 tablespoons (30 ml) agave nectar or maple syrup

1 tablespoon (16 g) tomato paste

½ cup (120 ml) raspberry or plain balsamic vinegar

½ cup (120 ml) red wine

½ cup (120 ml) water

1 clove garlic, minced

2 sprigs fresh rosemary

DIRECTIONS:

Add the blueberries, agave, tomato paste, vinegar, wine, water, and garlic to a blender and purée. Oil the crock of your slow cooker. Add the purée and the rosemary and cook on low for 3 to 4 hours, or on high for 1½ to 2 hours. (Many small slow cookers have no temperature control, so they cook everything on low.) Remove and discard the rosemary sprigs. Switch to warm or low to keep the sauce warm for a party.

Serve over vegan meatballs that have just come out of the oven, or keep the sauce in the slow cooker on warm and have the meatballs on the side for dipping.

YIELD: 12 servings
TOTAL PREP TIME: 15 minutes
TOTAL COOKING TIME: 3 to 4 hours on low or 1½ to 2 hours on high

A WORTHY NOTE

You can make the sauce the day before and keep it in the fridge until you are ready to reheat it for serving.

OLD-FASHIONED CEREAL SNACK MIX

When I was little one of my favorite things to make with my mom was Chex mix. I think the wheat Chex were the closest thing to health food in my family's pantry. Times change and my pantry is certainly much healthier than the one I grew up with, but I still love snack mix.

FOR THE SAUCE:

3 tablespoons (42 g) nondairy butter or (45 ml) olive oil

3 tablespoons (45 ml) vegan Worcestershire sauce

½ teaspoon garlic powder

½ teaspoon dried thyme

½ teaspoon paprika

¼ teaspoon celery seed

¼ teaspoon turmeric

Salt, to taste

INGREDIENTS:

6 cups* waffled unsweetened cereal, such as Chex (use a mixture of equal parts corn, rice, and wheat cereal, if possible)

*You need to measure the cereal by volume rather than weight in this recipe. This is because weight will vary greatly depending on the brand's density.

DIRECTIONS:

To make the sauce: Oil the crock of your slow cooker. Combine the sauce ingredients in the slow cooker and cook on high, covered, for 15 minutes, until the butter is melted. Add the cereal and stir to combine. Make sure your slow cooker is not more than three-fourths of the way full. The sauce will make the snack mix a little soggy, but the mixture will get crispy again as it cooks. Cook, uncovered, for 1 to 1½ hours, or until the mixture becomes crunchy again, stirring every 10 to 15 minutes to prevent burning.

YIELD: 8 to 10 servings
TOTAL PREP TIME: 5 minutes
TOTAL COOKING TIME: 1¼ to 1¾ hours

RECIPE IDEAS & VARIATIONS

Add your favorite extras to personalize your snack mix. My testers used mixed nuts, pretzels, and bagel chips. You can add them during cooking or after if you don't have room for them in your slow cooker.

SWEET AND SPICY NUT MIX

► SOY-FREE   ► GLUTEN-FREE

You catch a little heat at the end of this nut mix, but it's the sweet that you notice first.

....

FOR THE SAUCE:

¼ cup (60 ml) apple cider vinegar

2 tablespoons (30 ml) agave nectar or maple syrup

1 tablespoon (15 ml) olive oil

½ teaspoon cayenne pepper

½ teaspoon chipotle chile powder

¼ teaspoon garlic powder

¼ teaspoon paprika (regular or smoked)

INGREDIENTS:

4 cups* nuts of choice (I used cashews, pecans, and
   whole almonds)

*You need to measure the nuts by volume because the weight
will vary greatly depending on which nuts you choose.*

DIRECTIONS:

To make the sauce: Oil the crock of your slow cooker.
Whisk the sauce ingredients together in the slow cooker
until blended. Add the nuts and stir to coat. Make sure
your slow cooker is not more than three-fourths of the way
full. Cook on high, uncovered, for 1 to 1½ hours, or until the
nuts becomes crunchy, stirring every 10 to 15 minutes to
prevent burning.

YIELD: 6 to 8 servings
TOTAL PREP TIME: 5 minutes
TOTAL COOKING TIME: 1 to 1½ hours

RECIPE IDEAS & VARIATIONS

The recipe as it's written is medium hot. If you like
yours fiery, double the amount of chile powder.

PIMENTO CHEESE FONDUE

I grew up with sweet tea and grilled pimento cheese sandwiches. This is a way for vegans to enjoy cheesy goodness flecked with sweet, diced pimento. Serve it with veggies and toast points for dipping. Or serve over whole pieces of toast to make an English main dish called rarebit. The recipe is easy to double (or even triple), so it's great for a party.

Note: This recipe uses a 1½- to 2-quart (1.4 to 1.9 L) slow cooker. You can double or triple the recipe and use a larger slow cooker if you like.

INGREDIENTS:

1 can (15 ounces, or 420 g) white beans, drained and rinsed, or 1½ cups (340 g) homemade

¾ cup (180 ml) water

2 tablespoons (12 g) vegan chicken-flavored bouillon or 4 tablespoons (24 g) Chickeny Bouillon (page 19)

1 jar (2 ounces, or 56 g) diced pimentos, drained

2 cups (225 g) shredded vegan cheddar cheese

2 tablespoons (28 g) vegan mayonnaise or olive oil

½ teaspoon stone-ground mustard

Salt and pepper, to taste

DIRECTIONS:

Add the beans and the water to a food processor or blender and purée until smooth. Oil the crock of the slow cooker. Add the purée and the remaining ingredients and cook on low for 1 to 1½ hours, or until the cheese is fully melted. You will need to stir it a few times (about every 20 minutes) during cooking to fully incorporate the cheese as it melts.

If you prefer a thinner fondue, just add more water until it is the consistency that you desire.

YIELD: 4 servings
TOTAL PREP TIME: 10 minutes
TOTAL COOKING TIME: 1 to 1½ hours

SERVING SUGGESTION

Use leftovers as a sandwich filling, and grill your sandwich for a traditional Southern treat.

SUBTLY SPICY PEANUT COCONUT FONDUE

Peanut fondue is a perfect cocktail party dish. Serve with crispy pan-fried
tempeh strips, firm tofu cubes, tiny boiled potatoes, and lightly steamed veggies.
You can leave it in the slow cooker, and it will stay warm during your party.

*Note: This recipe uses a 1½- to 2-quart (1.4 to 1.9 L) slow
cooker. You can double or triple the recipe and use a larger
slow cooker if you like.*

INGREDIENTS:

½ cup (130 g) peanut butter

1 can (14 ounces, or 392 g) light coconut milk

1 clove garlic, minced

1½ tablespoons (12 g) fresh grated ginger

½ to 1 teaspoon soy sauce (to taste)

¼ to ½ teaspoon ground chile (chipotle, cayenne, etc.)

½ to 1 teaspoon garam masala

1 tablespoon (8 g) cornstarch, as needed

DIRECTIONS:

Oil the crock of your slow cooker. Combine the peanut
butter, coconut milk, garlic, ginger, soy sauce, ground chile,
and garam masala in the slow cooker. Cook on low for
1½ to 2 hours, or until the dip is heated through. If it's
too thin, add the cornstarch and cook 15 minutes longer.

YIELD: 4 servings
TOTAL PREP TIME: 10 minutes
TOTAL COOKING TIME: 1½ to 2 hours

SERVING SUGGESTION

Serve leftovers over rice and tofu for an easy meal.

SPINACH ARTICHOKE DIP

▸ SOY-FREE ▸ GLUTEN-FREE*

The cashew sour cream makes this dip thick and rich. This is the traditional
spinach artichoke dip that I ate a lot of when I lived in New Orleans,
only veganized. Serve with fresh veggies, crackers, or toast points.

INGREDIENTS:

2 tablespoons (30 ml) olive oil

1 small onion, minced

1 clove garlic, minced

8 cups (10 ounces, or 280 g) fresh baby spinach, washed

1 recipe Cashew Sour Cream (page 47)

Splash of water

1 can (14 ounces, or 392 g) artichoke hearts (packed in water, not marinated)

1/3 cup (37 g) nutritional yeast (*use gluten-free)

1/4 teaspoon smoked paprika or plain paprika and a few drops liquid smoke

1/4 teaspoon nutmeg (freshly grated, if possible)

Salt and pepper, to taste

DIRECTIONS:

Heat the oil in a skillet over medium heat and sauté the onion until translucent, 3 to 5 minutes. Add the garlic and spinach sauté until the spinach is reduced, 5 to 10 minutes.

Oil the crock of your slow cooker. Add the warm spinach mixture, cashew sour cream, water, artichokes, nutritional yeast, paprika, nutmeg, and salt and pepper and mix well. Cook on high for 30 minutes to 1 hour or on low for 1 to 1½ hours, until thoroughly heated through. Once hot, turn down the slow cooker to warm or low, and it will stay warm through the party. (Many small slow cookers have no temperature control, so they cook everything on low.) You may need to stir it every once in a while to prevent the top of the dip from turning brown and drying out.

YIELD: 8 servings
TOTAL PREP TIME: 15 minutes
TOTAL COOKING TIME: 1 to 1½ hours on low or 30 minutes to 1 hour on high

SERVING SUGGESTION

Serve leftovers as a topping for pasta. It's a grown-up mac and cheese variation.

CHEESY CHORIZO DIP

This is a spicy, thick, hearty dip for your chips. It's quick to throw together, and is ready to eat in less than 2 hours.

INGREDIENTS:

6 ounces (170 g) vegan chorizo

1 can (15 ounces, or 420 g) black beans, drained and rinsed, or 1½ cups (340 g) homemade (page 17)

1 can (14½ ounces, or 406 g) diced tomatoes or 1½ cups (340 g) fresh

1¼ cups (145 g) shredded vegan cheddar cheese

Salt, to taste

DIRECTIONS:

Oil the crock of your slow cooker. Add all the ingredients and cook on low for 1 to 1½ hours.

YIELD: 4 servings
TOTAL PREP TIME: 5 minutes
TOTAL COOKING TIME: 1 to 1½ hours

SERVING SUGGESTION

Try serving leftovers on top of baked potatoes or on pasta for a main course.

SMOKY BEAN DIP

When you find yourself with an impromptu party, you can make this dip with pantry staples. This one gets its flavor from the liquid smoke and cumin. You control just how spicy this will be by your choice of salsa. It goes great with baked blue tortilla chips and extra salsa on the side.

Note: This recipe uses a 1½- to 2-quart (1.4 to 1.9 L) slow cooker. You can double or triple the recipe and use a larger slow cooker if you like.

INGREDIENTS:

1 can (16 ounces, or 454 g) vegan refried beans or 1½ cups (340 g) homemade

½ cup (130 g) mild or spicy salsa

½ cup (58 g) shredded vegan cheddar cheese

2 to 6 drops liquid smoke (to taste)

½ teaspoon cumin

Salt, to taste

DIRECTIONS:

Oil the crock of your slow cooker. Add all the ingredients and cook on low for 1 to 1½ hours.

YIELD: 8 servings
TOTAL PREP TIME: 5 minutes
TOTAL COOKING TIME: 1 to 1½ hours

RECIPE IDEAS & VARIATIONS

No salsa? Substitute an equal amount of diced tomatoes (with or without green chiles).

CHAPTER 12

BREAKFASTS WORTH WAKING UP FOR

Every chilly morning, I have a hot breakfast waiting for me in my slow cooker. I'm a Southern girl, so grits are a part of my morning rotation, but oatmeal, quinoa, rice, and polenta work their way in, too.

It's also nice to have a fun, fancy weekend breakfast that can cook in less than 2 hours. Get a head start on your weekend, and put the Weekend Tofu and Hash Brown Casserole (page 196) or the Pear and Cardamom French Toast Casserole (page 197) on to cook. Then go do some yard work, errands, or simply read while it's cooking. These are perfect for a brunch get-together, too.

Many of these recipes call for a 1½- to 2-quart (1.4 to 1.9 L) slow cooker. If you are making breakfast for 2 or 3 people, it's the perfect size. It's inexpensive and you'll use it for dips and fondues, too, so it's worth getting one. You can always double or triple the recipe and use a larger slow cooker. But remember, your cooker needs to be half to three-fourths full.

Don't forget about coffee, tea, and spiced cider. All of them work great in the slow cooker, and are perfect for a large brunch. (And even better at a pumpkin-carving party!)

1. Maple-Sweetened Pumpkin-Spiced Latte
2. Cinnamon Spice Syrup
3. Do-It-Yourself Chai Concentrate
4. Pick-Your-Pleasure Breakfast Rice Pudding
5. Cranberry Vanilla Quinoa
6. Peach Almond Breakfast Polenta
7. Big Pot of Grits
8. Big Pot of Oatmeal
9. Pumpkin Pie Oatmeal
10. Carrot Cake and Zucchini Bread Oatmeal
11. Be-My-Valentine Chocolate Oatmeal
12. Scrambled Tofu with Peppers
13. Weekend Tofu and Hash Brown Breakfast Casserole
14. Pear and Cardamom French Toast Casserole
15. Maple Pecan Granola
16. Mixed Berry and Almond Granola

MAPLE-SWEETENED PUMPKIN-SPICED LATTE

▸ SOY-FREE ▸ GLUTEN-FREE

Fall comes around and hot drinks start seeming better, or at least as good as, the iced ones.
Wake up, throw all the ingredients into the slow cooker, and in 1½ to 2 hours you have
piping hot lattes made with the nondairy milk of your choice. Since you made this yourself,
you can walk around in your comfy sweater, and feel slightly smug as you watch the leaves fall.

Note: This recipe uses a 1½- to 2-quart (1.4 to 1.9 L) slow cooker. You can double or triple the recipe and use a larger slow cooker if you like.

INGREDIENTS:

1 to 2 cups (235 to 470 ml) brewed coffee or espresso
 (use more if you like stronger coffee flavor)

2 cups (470 ml) vanilla-flavored almond milk or nondairy
 milk mixed with 1 teaspoon vanilla extract

2 to 4 tablespoons (30 to 60 ml) maple syrup (to taste)

3 tablespoons (46 g) pumpkin purée, store-bought
 or homemade (page 34)

1 teaspoon cinnamon

¼ teaspoon ground cloves

¼ teaspoon allspice

⅛ teaspoon nutmeg

DIRECTIONS:

Place all the ingredients in the slow cooker. Whisk to combine. Cook on high for 1½ to 2 hours or on low for 3 hours. (Many small slow cookers have no temperature control, so they cook everything on low.) Stir well before serving because the pumpkin tends to settle at the bottom.

YIELD: 4 servings
TOTAL PREP TIME: 5 minutes
TOTAL COOKING TIME: 3 hours on low or 1½ to 2 hours on high

SERVING SUGGESTIONS

- Serve with whole cinnamon sticks for stirring. The pumpkin tends to sink to the bottom, so this a stylish way to stir it back together.

- If you have the time, purée the pumpkin with the nondairy milk in a blender. This will keep it from separating as much.

CINNAMON SPICE SYRUP

▸ SOY-FREE ▸ GLUTEN-FREE

This is a variation on a large coffee chain's syrup. It also goes great in tea, in apple cider, on crêpes, or with the Pear and Cardamom French Toast Casserole on page 197.

Note: This recipe uses a 1½- to 2-quart (1.4 to 1.9 L) slow cooker. You can double or triple the recipe and use a larger slow cooker if you like.

INGREDIENTS:

1 cup (235 ml) water

3 or 4 whole cinnamon sticks

6 whole cloves

¼ teaspoon allspice

⅛ teaspoon nutmeg

1 cup (225 g) packed brown sugar, (235 ml) agave nectar, or (235 ml) maple syrup

DIRECTIONS:

Combine the water, cinnamon, cloves, allspice, and nutmeg in the slow cooker. Whisk to combine. Cook on low for 5 to 8 hours. Strain out the cinnamon sticks and spices, stir in the brown sugar, then store in the fridge for 1 to 2 weeks.

YIELD: About 1 cup (235 ml)
TOTAL PREP TIME: 5 minutes
TOTAL COOKING TIME: 5 to 8 hours

SERVING SUGGESTION

Add 1 or 2 tablespoons (15 to 30 ml) to a cup of coffee, tea, or hot apple cider.

RECIPE IDEAS & VARIATIONS

- Make a gingerbread syrup by adding 4 slices fresh ginger and 2 tablespoons (40 g) molasses. Follow the same instructions.

- Want it to taste a little more like the fall drink from the coffee chain? Use brown sugar and increase the amount to 2 cups (450 g). All other ingredients and amounts stay the same.

DO-IT-YOURSELF CHAI CONCENTRATE

▸ SOY-FREE ▸ GLUTEN-FREE

I love chai, but it's getting pricey at coffee shops. It's well worth stocking up
on a few spices to make your own, and it's super easy, too. This one is exactly
the way I like it, but feel free to add more or less of some spices until it resembles
your favorite. If you like a licorice flavor, add one star anise—it creates a big flavor.

INGREDIENTS:

6 cups (1,410 ml) water

5 slices fresh ginger

7 whole cinnamon sticks

10 whole cloves

10 whole peppercorns

8 whole allspice berries

¼ teaspoon cardamom seeds

10 tea bags (black, green, or roobios)

½ to 1 cup (120 to 235 ml) agave nectar or maple
syrup (optional)

DIRECTIONS:

Combine the water and spices in the slow cooker. Cook
on low for 8 to 10 hours.

Add the tea bags to the slow cooker and turn up to high.
Let steep for 5 to 10 minutes, depending on how concen-
trated you want the flavor to be. Remove the tea bags and
add the agave.

Remove the cinnamon sticks. Pour into a pitcher while
straining out the spices through a piece of cheesecloth
placed in a funnel. Store in the fridge for 1 to 2 weeks.

YIELD: About 6 cup (1,410 ml)
TOTAL PREP TIME: 5 minutes
TOTAL COOKING TIME: 5 to 8 hours

SERVING SUGGESTION

Add ½ to 1 cup (120 to 235 ml) of the concentrate to
an equal amount nondairy milk. It's great hot or iced!

A WORTHY NOTE

You can put the spices in a muslin, reusable tea bag,
if you have one, and you won't have to strain it later.

PICK-YOUR-PLEASURE BREAKFAST RICE PUDDING

► SOY-FREE* ► GLUTEN-FREE

As much as I love my oatmeal, sometimes I need a change of pace. Nutritious brown rice cooks down into a creamy, sweet breakfast that's perfect to take to work in a thermos. Change out the flavorings and fruit to match your favorites. The combinations are endless! My favorite is vanilla extract with raisins.

Note: This recipe uses a 1½- to 2-quart (1.4 to 1.9 L) slow cooker. You can double or triple the recipe and use a larger slow cooker if you like.

INGREDIENTS:

½ cup (85 g) short- or long-grain brown rice

1 cup (235 ml) vanilla-flavored or plain nondairy milk (*use almond, hemp, rice, etc.)

1 cup (235 ml) water

½ teaspoon vanilla, almond, or orange extract

½ cup (60 g) dried cranberries or raisins** or chopped fresh apple or other fruit

2 tablespoons (30 g or ml) brown sugar, agave nectar, stevia, or maple syrup (or to taste)

**Some dried cranberries and raisins contain ascorbic acid. Ascorbic acid, like lemon juice, will curdle even nondairy milks. If yours contain it, cook with water instead of nondairy milk.

☽ THE NIGHT BEFORE:

Oil the crock of your slow cooker. Combine the rice, milk, water, extract, dried fruit (if using fresh, you can add it at the end), and brown sugar in the slow cooker. Cook on low for 6 to 8 hours.

☀ IN THE MORNING:

Stir the mixture and add more sweetener or liquid if needed. Top with fresh fruit if using.

YIELD: 2 large servings
TOTAL PREP TIME: 5 minutes
TOTAL COOKING TIME: 6 to 8 hours

CRANBERRY VANILLA QUINOA

▶ SOY-FREE ▶ GLUTEN-FREE

Quinoa is a nice change of pace from plain old oatmeal. And did you know that quinoa is not a grain, but a seed? Plus, it's a complete protein, so it's a perfect way to start your day.

Note: This recipe uses a 1½- to 2-quart (1.4 to 1.9 L) slow cooker. You can double or triple the recipe and use a larger slow cooker if you like.

INGREDIENTS:

½ cup (86 g) quinoa

2½ cups (588 ml) vanilla-flavored almond milk, plus more as needed

¼ cup (30 g) dried cranberries*

½ cup (123 g) unsweetened applesauce*

½ teaspoon vanilla extract (or scrape ¼ teaspoon vanilla paste from a split whole vanilla bean)

⅛ teaspoon stevia (optional)

Slivered almonds, for serving

Some dried cranberries and applesauces contain ascorbic acid. Ascorbic acid, like lemon juice, will curdle even nondairy milks. If yours contain it, cook with water instead of nondairy milk.

☾ THE NIGHT BEFORE:

Rinse the quinoa in a mesh strainer to remove the bitter coating. Oil the crock of your slow cooker. Combine the quinoa, millk, cranberries, applesauce, vanilla, and stevia in the slow cooker. Cook on low for 6 to 8 hours.

☼ IN THE MORNING:

Stir the quinoa, and taste and adjust the seasonings, or add more liquid. Top with the slivered almonds.

YIELD: 2 large servings
TOTAL PREP TIME: 5 minutes
TOTAL COOKING TIME: 6 to 8 hours

A WORTHY NOTE

Some quinoa is pre-rinsed, but some is not. If you are using a new to you brand always assume it is not rinsed, and rinse it yourself. There is nothing worse than throwing away a whole dish because it's too bitter to eat!

RECIPE IDEAS & VARIATIONS

Try switching out different flavors of apple or pear sauce, or using fruit butters or purées.

PEACH ALMOND BREAKFAST POLENTA

▶ SOY-FREE* ▶ GLUTEN-FREE**

Move over, cream of wheat, it's time to add polenta on the breakfast menu. This recipe has a similar consistency to cream of wheat. Try it the way I've written it (with almond meal and peaches), then make up your own variations. Try cooking up pear and ginger polenta or berries and basil polenta to take advantage of the freshest fruit of the season.

....

Note: This recipe uses a 1½- to 2-quart (1.4 to 1.9 L) slow cooker. You can double or triple the recipe and use a larger slow cooker if you like.

INGREDIENTS:

½ cup (70 g) polenta (**use gluten-free)

2 cups (470 ml) vanilla-flavored nondairy milk (*coconut, almond, rice, etc.)

¼ cup (25 g) almond meal

¼ cup (60 g) applesauce†

¼ teaspoon almond extract

2 sprigs thyme (optional)

2 large peaches, peeled, cored, and chopped

2 to 4 tablespoons (30 to 60 ml) agave nectar or maple syrup

Minced thyme, for topping (optional)

†Some applesauces contain ascorbic acid. Ascorbic acid, like lemon juice, will curdle even nondairy milks. If yours contain it, cook with water instead of nondairy milk.

☾ THE NIGHT BEFORE:

Oil the crock of your slow cooker. Combine the polenta, milk, almond meal, applesauce, almond extract, thyme sprigs, and peaches in the slow cooker. Cook on low for 6 to 8 hours.

☼ IN THE MORNING:

Remove the thyme sprigs. Stir the polenta and add the agave to taste. The amount of sweetener needed will vary with how sweet the peaches are. Top with extra minced thyme.

YIELD: 4 servings
TOTAL PREP TIME: 10 minutes
TOTAL COOKING TIME: 6 to 8 hours

RECIPE IDEAS & VARIATIONS

Pour leftovers into an oiled pan and chill. Once it has set up, cut into triangles. Grill the triangles until warm. Serve with fresh fruit and additional agave nectar or maple syrup for brunch or dessert.

BIG POT OF GRITS

▶ SOY-FREE ▶ GLUTEN-FREE

Grits are a staple in any Southern household. Everyone has his or her favorite variation. If you haven't tried grits before, don't be scared. They are very similar to polenta (in fact, the yellow ones *are* polenta).

Serve this at a brunch with an assortment of toppings, such as vegan bacon crumbles, vegan cheddar cheese, spicy pickled peppers, and roasted garlic. Everyone loves mix-ins.

INGREDIENTS:

1 cup (140 g) white or yellow grits

5 cups (1,175 ml) water

2 tablespoons (28 g) nondairy butter or 2 tablespoons (30 ml) olive oil

Salt and pepper, to taste

Shredded vegan cheddar cheese (optional)

☾ THE NIGHT BEFORE:

Oil the crock of your slow cooker. Combine the grits, water, butter, and salt and pepper in the slow cooker. Add more water if you will cook it longer the 8 hours or if your slow cooker runs a little hot. Cook on low for 6 to 10 hours.

☀ IN THE MORNING:

Taste and adjust the seasonings. Top with the cheese.

YIELD: 4 to 6 servings
TOTAL PREP TIME: 5 minutes
TOTAL COOKING TIME: 6 to 10 hours

RECIPE IDEAS & VARIATIONS

Try putting leftovers in a shallow oiled pan and store in the fridge. Later you can slice them into triangles and grill them. It makes a great meal topped with black beans and salsa.

A WORTHY NOTE

Contrary to popular belief, grits aren't just used in the South. If you are in an area where you can't easily buy grits, look for yellow polenta. Often they will be sub-labeled as corn grits.

BIG POT OF OATMEAL

▶ SOY-FREE* ▶ GLUTEN-FREE**

Oatmeal is underestimated in my opinion. It is full of nutrition, inexpensive, and as versatile as your imagination. Give it a little extra respect and feature it at your next brunch. Keep it warm in your slow cooker and add water as necessary to keep it loose. Set out a buffet of toppings, including fresh fruit, maple syrup, vanilla-flavored nondairy milk, chocolate shavings, toasted nuts, and dried fruit. It makes for a beautiful table and will satisfy your guests' appetites.

....

INGREDIENTS:

1 cup (80 g) steel-cut oats (**use gluten-free)

5 cups (1,175 ml) water

Vanilla-flavored nondairy milk (*use almond, rice, hemp, etc.), for serving

Fresh fruit or your favorite topping, for serving

☾ THE NIGHT BEFORE:

Oil the crock of your slow cooker. Add the oats and water to the slow cooker. Add more water if you will cook it longer than 8 hours or if your slow cooker runs a little hot. Cook on low for 6 to 10 hours.

☼ IN THE MORNING:

Stir the oatmeal to get a consistent texture. Serve in bowls topped with milk and fresh fruit.

YIELD: 6 servings
TOTAL PREP TIME: 5 minutes
TOTAL COOKING TIME: 6 to 10 hours

RECIPE IDEAS & VARIATIONS

If your slow cooker is older and cooks at a lower temperature use 4 cups (940 ml) of water instead of 5 cups (1,175 ml).

PUMPKIN PIE OATMEAL

▶ SOY-FREE ▶ GLUTEN-FREE*

I am addicted to winter squash. This oatmeal gets a nutritional boost
from the pumpkin, but still tastes like dessert for breakfast!

Note: This recipe uses a 1½- to 2-quart (1.4 to 1.9 L) slow cooker. You can double or triple the recipe and use a larger slow cooker if you like.

INGREDIENTS:

½ cup (40 g) steel-cut oats (*use gluten-free)

2 cups (470 ml) unsweetened vanilla-flavored almond milk

½ cup (125 g) pumpkin purée, store-bought or homemade (page 37)

½ teaspoon cinnamon

¼ teaspoon allspice

Pinch of ground cloves

Brown sugar, for serving

Chopped pecans, for serving

☾ THE NIGHT BEFORE:

Oil the crock of your slow cooker. Combine the oats, milk, pumpkin, cinnamon, allspice, and cloves in the slow cooker. Cook on low for 6 to 8 hours.

☀ IN THE MORNING:

Stir the oatmeal to get a consistent texture. Serve in bowls topped with brown sugar and pecans.

YIELD: 2 large servings
TOTAL PREP TIME: 5 minutes
TOTAL COOKING TIME: 6 to 8 hours

RECIPE IDEAS & VARIATIONS

You can use any winter squash you have on hand in place of the pumpkin. Try acorn or butternut—They are the closest in flavor.

CARROT CAKE AND ZUCCHINI BREAD OATMEAL

▶ SOY-FREE* ▶ GLUTEN-FREE**

This oatmeal is chock-full of veggies and takes elements from carrot cake and zucchini bread. If you're trying to get rid of your zucchini surplus, or just sneak in some veggies on the kids, this is the oatmeal for you. You can use only carrots, or only zucchini, but the combination is my favorite.

Note: This recipe uses a 1½- to 2-quart (1.4 to 1.9 L) slow cooker. You can double or triple the recipe and use a larger slow cooker if you like.

INGREDIENTS:

½ cup (40 g) steel-cut oats (**use gluten-free)

1½ cups (355 ml) vanilla-flavored nondairy milk (*use coconut, almond, rice, etc.)

1 small carrot, grated

¼ small zucchini, grated

Pinch of salt

Pinch of nutmeg

Pinch of ground cloves

½ teaspoon cinnamon

2 tablespoons (30 g or ml) brown sugar or maple syrup

¼ cup (28 g) chopped pecans

☪ THE NIGHT BEFORE:

Oil the crock of your slow cooker. Combine the oats, milk, carrot, zucchini, salt, nutmeg, cloves, cinnamon, and brown sugar in the slow cooker. Cook on low for 6 to 8 hours.

☀ IN THE MORNING:

Stir the oatmeal, taste and adjust the seasonings, and add more milk, if needed. Top with the chopped pecans.

YIELD: 2 large servings
TOTAL PREP TIME: 10 minutes
TOTAL COOKING TIME: 6 to 8 hours

A WORTHY NOTE

If you have picky eaters, you may want to peel the zucchini to get rid of any green specks they might notice.

BE-MY-VALENTINE CHOCOLATE OATMEAL

▸ SOY-FREE ▸ GLUTEN-FREE*

For Valentine's Day I wasn't sure what to get my other half. We were avoiding white sugar, so no chocolate hearts for us. I got creative and made us bowls of chocolate oatmeal. It tasted divine!

Note: This recipe uses a 1½- to 2-quart (1.4 to 1.9 L) slow cooker. You can double or triple the recipe and use a larger slow cooker if you like.

INGREDIENTS:

½ cup (40 g) steel-cut oats (*use gluten-free)

2 cups (470 ml) water

2 tablespoons (16 g) unsweetened cocoa powder

1 teaspoon vanilla extract

⅛ to ¼ teaspoon stevia (to taste)

½ cup (120 ml) unsweetened vanilla-flavored almond milk

1 tablespoon (15 ml) agave nectar (optional)

☾ THE NIGHT BEFORE:

Oil the crock of your slow cooker. Combine the oats, water, cocoa, vanilla, and stevia in the slow cooker. If you haven't used stevia before, you may want to start with ⅛ teaspoon and add more later. Stevia gets bitter as soon as you add too much. Cook on low for 6 to 8 hours.

☀ IN THE MORNING:

Stir the oatmeal and add the almond milk. Now you're ready to have some chocolate for breakfast! If you need an extra kick of sweet, go ahead and add the agave nectar.

YIELD: 2 large servings
TOTAL PREP TIME: 5 minutes
TOTAL COOKING TIME: 6 to 8 hours

RECIPE IDEAS & VARIATIONS

Add other favorites to the mix, such as peanut butter, almond butter, chopped walnuts, or anything else you like in your brownies or oatmeal. If you aren't a fan of dark chocolate, try using 1 tablespoon (8 g) of cocoa instead of 2 tablespoons (16 g).

SCRAMBLED TOFU WITH PEPPERS

▸ GLUTEN-FREE   ▸ OIL-FREE

Scrambled tofu doesn't take long to make on the stove top, so you may be wondering why it's in a slow cooker book. Imagine waking up in the morning and having breakfast waiting for you. That's the real reason to make this dish in the slow cooker. Vary the veggies with onions, broccoli, and carrots for a change of pace.

INGREDIENTS:

1 package (15 ounces, or 420 g) tofu, drained and crumbled

½ to 1 cup (120 to 235 ml) water

1 clove garlic, minced

½ bell pepper, chopped

1 teaspoon turmeric

½ teaspoon chili powder

Dash of liquid smoke (optional)

Dash of hot pepper sauce (optional)

Salt and pepper, to taste

Fresh herbs of choice, minced, for topping (optional)

Salsa, for topping (optional)

☾ THE NIGHT BEFORE:

Combine the tofu, water, garlic, bell pepper, turmeric, chili powder, liquid smoke, and hot sauce in the slow cooker. Add more water if you will cook it longer than 8 hours or if your slow cooker runs a little hot. Cook on low for 6 to 10 hours.

☀ IN THE MORNING:

Drain any excess water from the mixture. Season with salt and pepper and top with fresh herbs or salsa.

YIELD: 4 servings
TOTAL PREP TIME: 15 minutes
TOTAL COOKING TIME: 6 to 10 hours

RECIPE IDEAS & VARIATIONS

Add leftover veggies, black beans and salsa, or even diced onion to make your own variation.

WEEKEND TOFU AND HASH BROWN BREAKFAST CASSEROLE

▸ GLUTEN-FREE

This is a breakfast worth waiting for. Go do some yard work, take a walk, or just relax while your breakfast is cooking: cheesy potatoes covered with a light tofu custard.

INGREDIENTS:

1 package (16 ounces, or 454 g) frozen hash browns (no oil added, if possible)

½ cup (58 g) shredded vegan cheddar cheese

1 package (12 ounces, or 340 g) silken tofu

½ cup (120 ml) plain coconut creamer or other nondairy creamer or milk

2 tablespoons (12 g) vegan chicken-flavored bouillon or 4 tablespoons (24 g) Chickeny Bouillon (page 19)

¼ teaspoon turmeric

⅛ teaspoon garlic powder

½ teaspoon salt

Freshly ground pepper

Paprika, for sprinkling

DIRECTIONS:

Oil the crock of your slow cooker. Spread the frozen hash browns over the bottom of the slow cooker, then sprinkle the shredded cheese over them.

Place the tofu, creamer, bouillon, turmeric, garlic powder, and salt in a blender and blend until smooth. Pour the mixture over the hash browns. Sprinkle with freshly ground pepper and paprika.

Cook on high for 1½ to 2 hours. The custard will set up when done, but it will still be a little jiggly in the middle.

YIELD: 4 servings
TOTAL PREP TIME: 10 minutes
TOTAL COOKING TIME: 1½ to 2 hours

RECIPE IDEAS & VARIATIONS

Try adding a layer of vegan sausage, leftover pesto, or some Italian seasoning to keep it interesting.

PEAR AND CARDAMOM FRENCH TOAST CASSEROLE

This is similar to bread pudding in texture, but the sausage and fruit add
a breakfasty twist. Wake up and throw this together in the slow cooker. You'll have
time to take a walk or read the paper while it cooks. It's a perfect weekend treat.

INGREDIENTS:

4 links vegan breakfast sausages or 1 to 2 cups (110
to 220 g) crumbled precooked Apple Sage Sausage
(page 23)

3 medium-size pears

Juice of ½ lemon

½ loaf whole wheat bread, cubed (approximately
6 cups [300 g])

2 cups (470 ml) nondairy milk (plain, unsweetened,
or vanilla-flavored)

3 tablespoons (45 g) unsweetened applesauce (see note)

½ teaspoon cardamom

½ teaspoon cinnamon

Maple syrup, for serving

☪ **THE NIGHT BEFORE:**

If you are using link sausages, cut them into half-moons.
Cook the sausage in a nonstick skillet until done, 10 to
12 minutes. Peel and core the pears, then chop. Pour the
lemon juice over the pears to minimize browning. Store
the pears and sausage in an airtight container in the fridge.
Store the cubed bread in a resealable bag.

☼ **IN THE MORNING:**

Oil the crock of your slow cooker. Add the milk, applesauce, cardamom, and cinnamon and stir to combine.
Place the bread pears, and sausage on top, then press
down into the wet mixture.

Cook on high for 1½ to 2 hours. After 1 hour, press the
bread into the wet mixture again to help it cook more
thoroughly. Serve drizzled with maple syrup.

YIELD: 4 servings
TOTAL PREP TIME: 15 minutes
TOTAL COOKING TIME: 1½ to 2 hours

A WORTHY NOTE

Some applesauces contain ascorbic acid. Ascorbic
acid, like lemon juice, will curdle even nondairy
milks. If yours contains it, cook with water instead
of nondairy milk.

MAPLE PECAN GRANOLA

▸ SOY-FREE   ▸ GLUTEN-FREE*

Tired of burning granola when you make it in the oven? Making it in the slow cooker helps cook it just right. You still need to be around for a few hours to stir it, so it's perfect for a day when you are cooking other staples.

INGREDIENTS:

4 cups (320 g) rolled oats or multigrain rolled cereal (*use gluten-free)

1 cup (110 g) chopped pecans

3 tablespoons (21 g) ground flaxseed

¼ cup (60 ml) maple syrup or agave nectar mixed with 1 teaspoon maple extract

¼ cup (60 ml) olive oil

1 teaspoon vanilla extract

DIRECTIONS:

Oil the crock of your slow cooker. Add all the ingredients to the slow cooker and stir to combine. Cook on high, uncovered, for 3 to 4 hours, or until the oats are no longer soft and are a golden brown.

Stir every 15 to 20 minutes. You will need to stir every 10 minutes during the last hour. Let cool before storing or the condensation will make your granola soggy.

It's important to note that you cook this uncovered. I tried cooking it vented and it took longer than I was willing to wait. Uncovered, it cooks more quickly and is even easier to stir!

YIELD: 8 to 10 servings
TOTAL PREP TIME: 5 minutes
TOTAL COOKING TIME: 3 to 4 hours

MIXED BERRY AND ALMOND GRANOLA

▶ SOY-FREE ▶ GLUTEN-FREE*

I love to add sweet, crunchy granola to nondairy yogurt or ice cream.
I even eat it plain by the handfuls when I can't be bothered to fix myself
a proper breakfast. Use your favorite dried berries or raisins in this recipe.

INGREDIENTS:

3 cups (240 g) rolled oats (*use gluten-free)

½ cup (55 g) slivered almonds

½ cup (60 g) dried berry blend

3 tablespoons (21 g) ground flaxseed

¼ cup (60 ml) agave nectar

¼ cup (60 ml) olive oil

1 teaspoon almond or vanilla extract

¼ teaspoon cardamom

¼ teaspoon nutmeg

DIRECTIONS:

Oil the crock of your slow cooker. Add all the ingredients to the slow cooker and stir to combine. Cook on high, uncovered, for 3 to 4 hours, or until the oats are no longer soft and are a golden brown.

Stir every 15 to 20 minutes. You will need to stir every 10 minutes for the last hour. Let cool before storing or the condensation will make your granola soggy.

It's important to note that you cook this uncovered. I tried cooking it vented and it took longer than I was willing to wait. Uncovered, it cooks more quickly and is even easier to stir!

YIELD: 8 servings
TOTAL PREP TIME: 5 minutes
TOTAL COOKING TIME: 3 to 4 hours

RECIPE IDEAS & VARIATIONS

You can switch the extract to orange, add coconut, and sprinkle with a few mini chocolate chips for a super decadent treat.

CHAPTER 13

DECADENT DESSERTS AND DELIGHTFUL DRINKS

Desserts aren't the first thing you think of making when you buy a slow cooker, but almost every savvy cook ends up with one or two in his or her repertoire.

Poached pears and other cooked fruit are perfect in the slow cooker, plus they stay warm until you are ready to serve dessert, which is great for a multicourse dinner party. If your dinner party is in the winter, be sure to make Exotic Cardamom Hot Chocolate or Hot, Spiked, and Buttered Spiced Cider, both of which can be made in the slow cooker ahead of time.

Puddings, brownies, and blondies are also slow cooker favorites. Tapioca pudding has never been this easy. Just be sure to make it the night before so you can chill it in the fridge before serving. Try making some of your favorite brownie and blondie recipes in the slow cooker. If it's a fudgy mix, I recommend cooking it in an ovenproof pan that fits in your slow cooker. It's almost impossible to get very moist baked goods directly out of the crock in neat pieces.

1. Have-It-Your-Way Brownies
2. Tea "Thyme" Lemon Blondies
3. Chile-Chocolate Black Bean Brownies
4. Pumpkin Pie Pudding
5. Tapioca Pudding for Two
6. Mango Coconut Rice Pudding
7. Turkish Delight Tapioca Pudding
8. Earl Grey Poached Pears
9. Slightly Drunken Apples
10. Berrylicious Biscuit-Topped Fruit Cobbler
11. Hot, Spiked, and Buttered Spiced Cider
12. Exotic Cardamom Hot Chocolate

200

HAVE-IT-YOUR-WAY BROWNIES

▶ SOY-FREE*

I used a 6-quart (5.7 L) oval slow cooker and two small 3-cup (705 ml) rectanglular Pyrex dishes to make this recipe. You can use different sizes, but make sure the dishes you plan to use fit in your slow cooker before you start making the batter!

FOR THE DRY INGREDIENTS:

1 cup (120 g) whole wheat pastry flour

1 cup (120 g) unsweetened cocoa powder

½ teaspoon baking powder

¼ teaspoon salt

FOR THE WET INGREDIENTS:

½ cup (112 g) nondairy butter (*use olive oil)

½ cup (115 g) packed brown sugar

2 tablespoons (14 g) ground flaxseed mixed with 2 tablespoons (30 ml) warm water

1 cup (235 ml) plain or unsweetened vanilla-flavored nondairy milk (*use almond, rice, hemp, etc.)

1 teaspoon vanilla extract

DIRECTIONS:

To prepare the dry ingrdients: Combine the dry ingredients in a bowl and set aside.

To prepare the wet ingrdients: In a bowl or mixer, cream the butter with the brown sugar, then add the flaxseed mixture, milk, and vanilla. Mix until combined, then add half of the dry mixture and combine. Add the last of the dry mixture, combine well, and spread into the well-oiled dishes.

Take a piece of aluminum foil, roll it up, make a ring with it, and place on the bottom of the slow cooker. Put the baking dishes on top of the foil ring. (I arranged one dish crisscrossed over the other on top of the aluminum foil ring.) Place a clean dish towel underneath the lid to catch the condensation. Cook on high for 4 to 5 hours, or until a knife inserted into the center comes out almost clean.

YIELD: 12 pieces
TOTAL PREP TIME: 20 minutes
TOTAL COOKING TIME: 4 to 5 hours

RECIPE IDEAS & VARIATIONS

Make this recipe and embellish it with all your favorites, such as chocolate chips, nuts, and other goodies.

TEA "THYME" LEMON BLONDIES

▶ SOY-FREE*

These are super moist and full of lemony goodness. If you're not a fan of thyme you can leave it out, or try it with rosemary if you're feeling adventurous.

....

FOR THE DRY INGREDIENTS:

¾ cup (150 g) sugar

2 cups (240 g) whole wheat pastry flour

1 teaspoon dried thyme

1 teaspoon baking powder

½ teaspoon baking soda

½ teaspoon salt

FOR THE WET INGREDIENTS:

¾ cup (355 ml) vanilla-flavored nondairy milk (*use almond, rice, hemp, etc.) or plain nondairy milk mixed with ½ teaspoon vanilla extract

Zest of 1 lemon

Juice of 2 lemons

3 tablespoons (45 ml) olive oil

1 tablespoon (15 ml) almond-flavored liqueur or ½ teaspoon almond extract

1 teaspoon lemon or orange extract

DIRECTIONS:

To prepare the dry ingredients: Combine all the dry ingredients in a large bowl.

To prepare the wet ingredients: Combine all the wet ingredients in a separate bowl. Add the wet mixture to the dry and stir with a wooden spoon until just combined.

Pour into an oiled pan that fits in your slow cooker. If you have a round slow cooker, you can use a round dish (about 1-quart (0.9 L) size) or a loaf pan, or cook directly in the oiled crock. Prop the lid open with a wooden spoon to allow the condensation to evaporate. Cook on high until a knife inserted into the center comes out almost clean, 1½ to 2½ hours.

YIELD: 1 loaf
TOTAL PREP TIME: 15 minutes
TOTAL COOKING TIME: 1½ to 2½ hours

A WORTHY NOTE

If you cook this directly in the crock, rotate the crock two or three times during cooking. This way, if your slow cooker has a side that cooks hotter, your blondies will cook more evenly.

CHILE-CHOCOLATE BLACK BEAN BROWNIES

▶ SOY-FREE ▶ GLUTEN-FREE*

These healthy brownies are extremely fudgey and moist. Lining your baking dishes with parchment paper will help you pull the entire cooked contents out of the slow cooker and pan. It will be very hard, maybe impossible, to get the brownies out of the dish in one piece if you skip this step.

I used a 6-quart (5.7 L) oval slow cooker and two small 3-cup (705 ml) rectanglular Pyrex dishes to make this recipe. You can use different sizes, but make sure the dishes you plan to use fit in your slow cooker before you start making the batter!

INGREDIENTS:

½ cup (40 g) rolled oats (*use gluten-free)

½ cup (60 g) chopped walnuts

1 can (15 ounces, or 420 g) black beans, drained and rinsed, or 1½ cups (340 g) homemade (page 17)

2 ripe bananas

3 tablespoons (45 g) applesauce

¼ cup (60 ml) agave nectar or maple syrup

½ cup (60 g) unsweetened cocoa powder

¼ teaspoon chile powder (cayenne or chipotle are my favorites)

½ teaspoon cinnamon

1 teaspoon vanilla extract

RECIPE IDEAS & VARIATIONS

If you are making this for kids, leave out the chile powder and add a few more tablespoons (30 to 45 ml) agave nectar to make them sweeter. You can also leave out the cinnamon and add some mint extract instead. In other words, customize the recipe to fit your family's comfort zone.

☪ THE NIGHT BEFORE:

Process the rolled oats in a food processor to a flourlike consistency. (You can substitute instant oatmeal instead if you have it on hand.) Remove the oats and put in a large mixing bowl with the walnuts. Add the beans, bananas, applesauce, agave, cocoa, chile powder, cinnamon, and vanilla to the food processor and process until smooth. Add this mixture to the mixing bowl with the oats and stir to combine.

Line the baking dishes with parchment paper, cut long enough to hang over the edge of the pan. Spoon the brownie mixture over it. You will need to push it into the corners or your brownies won't have the shape you're expecting. Cover and store in the fridge.

☼ IN THE MORNING:

Roll up some aluminum foil, make a ring with it, and place in the bottom of the slow cooker. Put the baking dishes on top of the foil ring. (I arranged one dish crisscrossed over the other on top of the aluminum foil ring.) Place a clean dish towel underneath the lid to catch the condensation. Cook on low for 6 to 8 hours.

YIELD: 12 pieces
TOTAL PREP TIME: 20 minutes
TOTAL COOKING TIME: 6 to 8 hours

PUMPKIN PIE PUDDING

▶ GLUTEN-FREE

This tastes just like pumpkin pie. It's perfect for those times you have a gluten-intolerant guest (or a crust hater, like my friend Christy) over for dinner.

INGREDIENTS:

9½ ounces (270 g) firm tofu (about ½ package)

2½ cups (613 g) pumpkin purée, store-bought or homemade (page 34)

½ cup (120 ml) maple syrup

2 tablespoons (30 g) packed brown sugar

1 teaspoon cinnamon

½ teaspoon allspice

⅛ teaspoon ground ginger

⅛ teaspoon ground cloves

DIRECTIONS:

Add all the ingredients to a blender or food processor and purée until smooth. Pour into an oiled crock and cook on low for 5 to 6 hours or on high for 2½ to 3 hours. You can tell when it's ready because the top will stop being jiggly and crack a bit, just like a baked pumpkin pie.

Scoop into serving bowls and serve warm or chilled.

YIELD: 6 servings
TOTAL PREP TIME: 15 minutes
TOTAL COOKING TIME: 5 to 6 hours on low or 2½ to 3 hours on high

SERVING SUGGESTION

Make a topping bar by using small bowls on a tray to bring to the table when you serve this pudding. Offer granola, chopped nuts, vegan marshmallows, or even candied cranberries.

TAPIOCA PUDDING FOR TWO

▶ SOY-FREE* ▶ GLUTEN-FREE

Sometimes I don't want to have leftover dessert to tempt me. This makes just the right amount for two people. Make it the night before to have dessert after dinner the next night.

Note: This recipe uses a 1½- to 2-quart (1.4 to 1.9 L) slow cooker. You can double or triple the recipe and use a larger slow cooker if you like.

INGREDIENTS:

2 cups (470 ml) plain or unsweetened nondairy milk (*use almond, hemp, oat, etc.)

¼ cup (38 g) tapioca pearls (not soaked)

¼ cup (50 g) sugar

1 teaspoon vanilla extract

Pinch of salt

DIRECTIONS:

Oil the crock of your slow cooker. Add all the ingredients and cook for 3 hours on low or 1½ hours on high. Stir and transfer to a container to cool for 1 hour, then put in the fridge overnight. The pudding will still seem very runny, but it will set up in the fridge.

YIELD: 2 large servings
TOTAL PREP TIME: 5 minutes
TOTAL COOKING TIME: 3 hours on low or 1½ hours on high

RECIPE IDEAS & VARIATIONS

You don't need to have "Plain Jane" tapioca just because you're showing some restraint. Try adding in a few drops of almond extract or orange flower water in place of the vanilla. Of course, you can always add dried fruit, applesauce, or even a few chocolate chips.

MANGO COCONUT RICE PUDDING

▸ SOY-FREE* ▸ GLUTEN-FREE

This recipe is reminiscent of mango sticky rice. Coconut milk adds creaminess while mango adds a burst of fruit flavor to the mix. I like to use light coconut milk, but regular will work fine, too.

INGREDIENTS:

2 mangoes, peeled and diced (see page 77)

1½ cups (280 g) Arborio rice

1 can (14 ounces, or 392 g) light coconut milk

1½ cups (355 ml) vanilla-flavored nondairy milk (*use almond, rice, hemp, etc.), plus more as needed

½ cup (100 g) sugar or (120 ml) maple syrup or agave nectar

1 teaspoon vanilla extract

DIRECTIONS:

Oil the crock of your slow cooker. Add all the ingredients and cook on high for 1½ to 2 hours. Add a little more non-dairy milk if the mixture is not wet or creamy enough.

YIELD: 8 servings
TOTAL PREP TIME: 15 minutes
TOTAL COOKING TIME: 1½ to 2 hours

SERVING SUGGESTION

This is a perfect dessert for a dinner party. Prep the ingredients ahead of time, then start cooking when you sit down to dinner, and dessert will be ready by the time you are! Top with more fresh mango slices and some shredded coconut to show off.

TURKISH DELIGHT TAPIOCA PUDDING

▶ SOY-FREE* ▶ GLUTEN-FREE

Turkish delight is a gel candy from the Middle East. Although it comes in many flavors, my favorite is rosewater. This pudding has that wonderful sweet floral flavor in a pudding that's textured with tapioca pearls.

INGREDIENTS:

4 cups (940 ml) plain or unsweetened nondairy milk (*use almond, hemp, oat, etc.)

1/2 cup (75 g) tapioca pearls (not soaked)

1/2 cup (100 g) sugar

Pinch of salt

1 teaspoon rosewater (make sure it is labeled food grade)

DIRECTIONS:

Oil the crock of your slow cooker. Add the milk, tapioca, sugar, and salt to the slow cooker. Cook for 3 1/2 hours on low or 2 hours on high. Stir in the rosewater and transfer to a container to cool for 1 hour, then put in the fridge overnight. The pudding will still seem very runny, but it will set up in the fridge.

YIELD: 6 servings
TOTAL PREP TIME: 5 minutes
TOTAL COOKING TIME: 3 1/2 hours on low or 2 hours on high

A WORTHY NOTE

This recipe works fine in a 4-quart (3.8 L) slow cooker; however, you should double it if you a using a 6 quart (5.7 L).

EARL GREY POACHED PEARS

▸ SOY-FREE ▸ GLUTEN-FREE

I have always admired poached pears, and I always thought of then as
the ultimate grown-up dessert. Peeled and left whole they add a bit of drama to a
dinner party. Chopped up, they make a perfect topping for nondairy vanilla ice cream.
These are poached in Earl Grey tea sweetened with brown sugar. The flavor is reminiscent
of a floral caramel. In fact, you could take the leftover poaching liquid and reduce it on
the stove until it's thicker and add it to coffee or tea, or top some other dessert with it.

INGREDIENTS:

4 pears, peeled, left whole or cored and chopped

1 cup (235 ml) Earl Grey tea (steep 1 tablespoon [4 g]
    tea in 1 cup [235 ml] hot water for 4 minutes)

$\frac{1}{2}$ cup (115 g) brown sugar

$\frac{1}{2}$ vanilla bean, scraped, or 1 teaspoon vanilla extract

Pinch of salt

DIRECTIONS:

Place the pears in the slow cooker. Combine the tea,
sugar, vanilla, and salt in a bowl and then pour over the
pears. Cook on high for 1$\frac{1}{2}$ to 2$\frac{1}{2}$ hours. If you are using
whole pears place them on their sides and turn them
every 30 minutes.

YIELD: 4 servings
TOTAL PREP TIME: 15 minutes
TOTAL COOKING TIME: 1$\frac{1}{2}$ to 2$\frac{1}{2}$ hours

RECIPE IDEAS & VARIATIONS

If you are avoiding refined sugar, use maple syrup
or agave nectar instead of the brown sugar. Another
option is to use heated fruit juice instead of water to
brew the tea.

SLIGHTLY DRUNKEN APPLES

▶ SOY-FREE   ▶ GLUTEN-FREE

Sometimes you just need to top off your day with dessert. The rum and liqueur add extra flavor, but if you don't imbibe feel free to substitute with water or apple juice.

....

Note: This recipe uses a 1½- to 2-quart (1.4 to 1.9 L) slow cooker or a small ovenproof dish in a larger slow cooker. You can double or triple the recipe and use a larger slow cooker if you like.

INGREDIENTS:

4 apples, peeled if not organic, cored, and sliced

1 tablespoon (15 g) brown sugar

Juice of 2 or 3 tangerines

Juice of ½ lime or lemon

3 tablespoons (45 ml) rum (optional)

1½ tablespoons (23 ml) Navan, Amaretto, or Triple Sec (optional)

½ teaspoon ground ginger

½ teaspoon dried marjoram or basil (or 1 teaspoon fresh added right before serving)

DIRECTIONS:

Place the apples in the slow cooker. Combine the brown sugar, tangerine and lime juices, rum, Navan, ginger, and marjoram in a small bowl and then pour over the apples. Cook on low for 6 to 8 hours. (Many small slow cookers have no temperature control, so they cook everything on low.)

YIELD: 4 servings
TOTAL PREP TIME: 15 minutes
TOTAL COOKING TIME: 6 to 8 hours

SERVING SUGGESTION

Serve by itself, with nondairy creamer poured over the top, over low-fat nondairy vanilla ice cream, or on your oatmeal for a special treat.

BERRYLICIOUS BISCUIT-TOPPED FRUIT COBBLER

This is one of my favorite slow cooker desserts. You can use any fresh
or frozen fruit you have on hand. It's easy to make and a real crowd-pleaser.
You can use agave nectar or maple syrup instead of white sugar, if you prefer.

FOR THE STEWED FRUIT:

1 pint (340 g) berries (blueberries, strawberries,
    raspberries, or blackberries), washed, stemmed,
    hulled if strawberries, and chopped if large

5 large apples, peeled and cored

1 tablespoon (15 ml) lemon juice

1 teaspoon lemon zest

1/2 cup (100 g) sugar

1 tablespoon (8 g) cornstarch

Pinch of salt

FOR THE BISCUITS:

1 1/2 cups (180 g) flour (white, whole wheat, or
    gluten-free baking mix)

1/2 cup (50 g) oat bran

1/3 cup (67 g) sugar

1 1/2 teaspoons baking powder

Pinch of salt

3 tablespoons (45 ml) olive oil

1/2 cup (120 ml) plain or unsweetened nondairy milk

1 teaspoon vanilla extract

DIRECTIONS:

To make the stewed fruit: Oil the crock of your slow
cooker. Combine all of the ingredients in the slow cooker.
Add 1/2 cup (120 ml) water if you will cook it longer than
8 hours or if your slow cooker runs very hot. Cook on low
for 6 to 8 hours.

About 30 minutes before serving: Add a little water if
the mixture is too thick, or add an additional 1/2 teaspoon
cornstarch if it needs to thicken up a bit.

To make the biscuits: Combine the flour, oat bran, sugar,
baking powder, and salt in a bowl. In a separate bowl,
combine the oil, milk, and vanilla. Add the dry ingredients
to the wet and stir with a wooden spoon to combine. Turn
the mixture out onto a floured cutting board, roll out about
1/2 inch (1.3 cm) thick, and cut into circles with a glass.

Place in the slow cooker on top of the filling, turn up the
slow cooker to high, and prop the lid open with a wooden
spoon to allow the condensation to evaporate. Cook for
30 minutes longer. Scoop out into bowls for serving.

YIELD: 4 to 6 servings
TOTAL PREP TIME: 30 minutes
TOTAL COOKING TIME: 6 to 8 hours plus 30 minutes to
cook the biscuit crust

RECIPE IDEAS & VARIATIONS

You can substitute any in-season fruit and make this
any day of the year. Try peach and raspberry, or pear
and apple. Jazz up the cobbler by mixing minced
mint, thyme, or rosemary into the biscuit dough.

HOT, SPIKED, AND BUTTERED SPICED CIDER

▶ SOY-FREE* ▶ GLUTEN-FREE**

There's no need to choose between spiced cider and hot buttered rum
when you can have it all in one mug. Make it to your liking by leaving
out the rum or nondairy butter, or use apple juice instead of cider.

INGREDIENTS:

4 cups (940 ml) apple cider

2 cinnamon sticks

4 cardamom pods

3 allspice berries

4 whole cloves

4 teaspoons (20 g) nondairy butter
(use *soy-free or **gluten-free)

½ to ¾ cup (120 to 180 ml) rum

DIRECTIONS:

Combine all the ingredients in the slow cooker. You can
also wait and add the rum to the mugs right before serving
if everyone isn't imbibing. Cook on low for 2 to 4 hours.
Strain out the cinnamon, cardamom, allspice, and cloves.
Stir well before serving in mugs garnished with extra cinnamon sticks.

YIELD: 4 servings
TOTAL PREP TIME: 5 minutes
TOTAL COOKING TIME: 2 to 4 hours

A WORTHY NOTE

You can halve this recipe for 2 servings and cook in
a 1½-quart (1.4 L) slow cooker.

EXOTIC CARDAMOM HOT CHOCOLATE

▸ SOY-FREE   ▸ GLUTEN-FREE

Who needs cake or cookies when all you have to do is ladle yourself a warm mug of extra-thick, sweetly spiced hot chocolate from the slow cooker? Throw this together before dinner and you'll have a sweet treat before you go to bed. You can halve this recipe for 2 or 3 servings and cook in a 1½-quart (1.4 L) slow cooker.

INGREDIENTS:

4 cups (940 ml) unsweetened vanilla almond milk or plain almond milk mixed with 1 teaspoon vanilla extract

3 ounces (84 g) semisweet chocolate disks or bars, coarsely chopped

¼ to ½ cup (50 to 100 g) sugar

12 whole cardamom pods

2 cinnamon sticks (optional)

4 to 6 vegan marshmallows, for serving (optional)

DIRECTIONS:

Combine the milk, chocolate, sugar, cardamom, and cinnamon in the slow cooker. Cook on low for 2 to 3 hours, whisking every 30 minutes, or until all the chocolate is melted. Strain out the cardamom and cinnamon. Stir well before serving in mugs, topped with a vegan marshmallow.

YIELD: 4 to 6 servings
TOTAL PREP TIME: 5 minutes
TOTAL COOKING TIME: 2 to 3 hours

RECIPE IDEAS & VARIATIONS

- If you are avoiding refined sugar, use unsweetened chocolate instead of the semisweet, and replace the sugar with a natural sweetener of your choice, such as stevia, agave nectar, or maple syrup.

- Omit the spices for a traditional hot chocolate. Or add some mint extract or 2 herbal peppermint tea bags for a peppermint chocolate treat.

ACKNOWLEDGMENTS

This book would not exist if it weren't for the help of all the people behind the scenes. I want to especially thank Amanda Waddell and Will Kiester at Fair Winds Press. This would not have been possible without your patience and support.

Thanks to Karen Levy and Betsy Gammons for being so easy to work with and doing a great editing job. I am very grateful to the designers Nancy Bradham, Megan Jones, and Meg Sniegoski for creating such an amazing design for this book. The beautiful photography is the work of photographer Bill Bettencourt and food stylist, Steve Fugikawa.

Special thanks to all my testers and their willingness to cook anything, even if they didn't think it could be done in a slow cooker. Their dedication and detailed feedback made this a better book.

Much gratitude to all my friends who taste tested for me, encouraged me, and managed not to make too much fun of just how many slow cookers I was acquiring in the process of writing this book.

Many thanks to both Dawn Meisch and Ellen Foreman who checked and edited all the recipes before my deadlines to put me at ease. They were my cheerleaders throughout the entire book process.

I can't possibly thank Cheryl Purser enough for taking care of me, the animals, and our home while I was busier than I thought possible writing this book. She even tried all the food, even though she is a super picky eater!

ABOUT THE AUTHOR

Kathy Hester lives in Durham, North Carolina, with her two cats (that would rather not live together), a cute dog with a belly-rubbing addiction, her very own picky eater, a kitchen garden, and more slow cookers than one person should own.

Kathy writes a vegan slow cooker blog, www.healthyslowcooking.com, and posts a variety of other vegan recipes, on her blog, *Busy Vegan*, www.busyvegan.com. When she's not blogging, she writes articles about food, menu planning, and cooking for picky eaters for a variety of websites such as EverythingMom, www.everythingmom.com.

INDEX